FREEDOMPRENEURS.CLUB

COPYRIGHT AND DISCLAIMER

This material is copyright. No part, in whole or in part, may be reproduced by any process, or any other exclusive right exercised, without the permission of www.HangOutWithCoachNick.com © 2014

NICK PEREIRA

Published by:
Leader Publishing Worldwide
19 Axford Bay
Port Moody, BC V3H 3R4
Tel: 1 888 294 9151
Fax: 1 877 575 9151
Website: www.noresults-nofee.com

DISCLAIMER AND/OR LEGAL NOTICES:
While every attempt has been made to verify information provided in this book, neither the author nor the publisher assumes any responsibility for any errors, omissions or inaccuracies.

Any slights of people or organizations are unintentional. If advice concerning legal or related matters is needed, the services of a qualified professional should be sought. This book is not intended as a source of legal or accounting advice. You should be aware of any laws which govern business transactions or other business practices in your state or province.

The income statements and examples are not intended to represent or guarantee that everyone will achieve the same results. Each individual's success will be determined by his or her desire, dedication, effort, and motivation. There are no guarantees you will duplicate the results stated here, you recognize that any business endeavor has inherent risk for loss of capital.

Any reference to any persons or business, whether living or deceased, existing or defunct, is purely coincidental.

PRINTED 2016

DEDICATION

I would like to dedicate this book to all the brave souls who have unplugged from the matrix and who are carving their own path and following their dreams.

To Your Success,

Nick Pereira

CONTENTS

Chapter 01	...	Use Goal Setting Effectively
Chapter 02	...	How to Profit through Time Management
Chapter 03	...	Define Your Target Market
Chapter 04	...	Creating a Powerful Offer
Chapter 05	...	Immediate Sales
Chapter 06	...	Profiting from Internet Marketing
Chapter 07	...	Copywriting for Profits
Chapter 08	...	How to create repeat business
Chapter 09	...	How to Use Testimonials and Profit from Social Proof
Chapter 10	...	Systemizing Your Business and Developing Effective Processes

INTRODUCTION

This is the first page, but by opening this book you have already taken an important step towards increasing the success of your mission and becoming a freedompreneur. Congratulations in your quest to enhance your business and marketing skills so you can live the lifestyle you deserve.

When I put pen to paper or keyboard to word document, I found myself with an enormous amount of useful marketing material I've used since I was 17 years old. This experience is drawn from many different entrepreneurial ventures including selling ceramics in a flea market; ownership and management of a commercial cleaning company; the direct sales and network marketing industry; IT sales for a cloud based software, and of course, my coaching and training business where I have used this experience and knowledge to help thousands of coaches and healers become freedompreneurs. The strategies I talk about in this book are still in place at these businesses and I use them every single day coaching coaches, healers, light workers and conscious warriors of all walks of life and disciplines.

Even though I truly believe we are all one or two great marketing ideas away from more sales opportunities than we can fully imagine, I believe the first two chapters are as important as the following eight. The strategies in this book - when implemented with intention and care - are guaranteed to make help you create a larger impact and grow your income. These are strategies that have helped coaches and healers just like you make hundreds of thousands of dollars while working less hours.

This is the reason I have dedicated my life to coaching and training entrepreneurs. Since starting in business I wanted to plug into simple, proven systems that will me be successful while maintaining what is truly important to me. My relationship with the divine, my family and the people I am here to serve. I have been literally overwhelmed with the demand for marketing, structure, accountability and for the need to have like-minded conscious business owners surrounding themselves with someone that cares and to provide a proper and profitable third party perspective.

As you follow the book and read the principles to follow, remember it does not matter what industry nor type of business you operate (I've been part of many). What matters is that you grasp the heart of the principles, the underlying lessons and strategies, that can help grow any operation in any category of business imaginable.

The best time to start is NOW, not tomorrow, not next week or next year.

To Your Success,

Coach Nick

PS. If you would like to arrange a meeting to get a profitable third party perspective on your business, please send an email to support@hangoutwithcoachnick.com and I will gladly point you in the right direction.

For a Free Test Drive of all my best tips, tricks and marketing resources visit www.HangOutWithCoachNick.com

1

Use Goal Setting Effectively

We've all heard about the power of setting goals. Everyone has surely seen statistics that connect goal setting to success in both your business life, and your personal life. I'm sure if I asked you today what your goals are, you could rattle off a few wants and hopes without thinking too long.

However, what most people do not realize is that the power of goal setting lies in *writing goals down*. Committing goals to paper and reviewing them regularly gives you a 95% higher chance of achieving your desired outcomes. Studies have shown that only three to five percent of people in the world have written goals – the same three to five percent who have achieved success in business and make considerable impact.

These studies have also found that by retirement, only four per cent of people in the world will have enough accumulated wealth to maintain their income level, and quality of life. As a business owner, it is essential that you develop a plan for your retirement, but it is equally essential that you develop a plan for your success.

This chapter focuses on the power of goal setting as part of your business success. We'll teach you to set SMART goals that are rooted in your own personal value system, and supporting techniques to achieve your goals faster.

What are Goals?

Goals are clear targets that are attached to a specific time frame and action plan; they focus your efforts, and drive your motivation in a clear direction. Goals are different from dreams in that they outline a plan of action, while dreams are a conceptual vision of your wish or desired outcome.

Goals require work; work on yourself, work for your business, and work for others. You cannot achieve a goal – no matter how badly you want it – without being prepared to make a considerable effort. If you are ready to invest your time and energy, goals will help you to:

- Realize a dream or wish for your personal or business life
- Make a change in your life – add positive, or remove negative
- Improve your skills and performance ability
- Start or change a habit – positive or negative

Why Set Goals?

As we've already reviewed, setting goals and committing them to paper is the most effective way to cultivate success. The most important reason to set a goal is **to attach a clear action plan to a desired outcome.**

Goals help focus our time and energy on one (or several) key outcomes at a time. Many coaches and healers have hundreds of ideas whirring around in their heads at any one time, on top of daily responsibilities. By writing down and focusing on a few ideas at a time, you can prioritize and concentrate your efforts, avoid being stretched too thin, and produce greater results.

Since goals attach action to outcomes, goals can help to break down big dreams into manageable (and achievable) sections. Creating a multi-goal strategy will put a road map in place to help you get to your desired outcome. If your goal is to make six figures a year, there are a number of smaller steps to achieve before you achieve your end result.

Success doesn't happen by itself. It is the result of consistent and committed action by an individual who is driven to achieve something. Success means something different for everyone, so creating goals is a personal endeavor. Goals can be large and small, personal and public, financial and spiritual. It is not the size of the goal that matters; what matters is that you write the goal down and commit to making the effort required to achieve it.

What happens when I achieve a goal?

You should congratulate yourself and your team, of course! By rewarding yourself and your team (and clients) after every achievement, you not only train your mind to associate hard work with reward, but develop loyalty among your team and clients.

You should also ask yourself if your achievement can be taken to the next level, or if your goal can be stretched by building on the effort you have already made. Consistently setting new and higher targets will lay the framework for constant improvement and personal and professional growth.

Power of Positive Thinking

When was the last time you tuned into your internal stream of consciousness? What does the stream of thoughts that run through your mind sound like? Are they positive? Negative? Are they logical? Reasonable?

Positive thinking and healthy self-talk are the most important business tools you can ever cultivate; by programming a positive stream of subconscious thoughts into your mind, you can control your reality, and ultimately your goals. Think about someone you know who is constantly negative; someone who complains and whines and makes excuses for their unhappiness. How successful are they? How do their fears and doubts become reality in their world?

You are what you continuously believe about yourself and your environment. If you focus your mind on something in your mental world, it will nearly always manifest as reality in your physical world.

Positive thinking is a key part of setting goals. You won't achieve your goal until you believe that you can. You will achieve your goals faster when you believe in yourself, and the people around you who are helping to make your goal a reality.

Successful people are rooted in a strong belief system – belief in themselves, belief in the work they are doing, and belief in the people around them. They are motivated to improve and learn, but also confident in their existing skills and knowledge. Their positive attitude and energy is clearly felt in everything they do.

Ever notice how complainers usually surround themselves with other complainers? The same is true of positive thinkers. If you cultivate an upbeat and positive attitude, you will be surrounded by people who share your values and outlook on life.

Too often, people and our society subscribe to a continuous stream of negative chatter. The more you hear it, the more you'll believe it.

How many times have you heard:

- That's impossible.
- Don't even bother.
- It's already been done.
- We tried that, and it didn't work.
- You're too young.
- You're too old.
- You'll never get there.
- You'll never get that done.
- You can't do that.

Positive thinking and positive influences will provide the support you need to achieve your goals. Choose your friends and close colleagues wisely, and surround yourself with positive thinkers.

Creating SMART Goals

SMART goals are just that: smart. Whether you are setting goals for your personal life, your business, or with your employees, goals that have been developed with the SMART principle have a higher probability of being achieved.

The SMART Principle

1. Specific

Specific goals are clearer and easier to achieve than nonspecific goals. When writing down your goal, ask yourself the five "W" questions to narrow in on what exactly you are aiming for. Who? Where? What? When? Why?

For example, instead of a nonspecific goal like, "get in shape for the summer," a specific goal would be, "go to the gym three times a week and eat twice as many vegetables."

2. Measurable

If you can't measure your goal, how will you know when you've achieved it? Measurable goals help you clearly see where you are, and where you want to be. You can see change happen as it happens.

Measurable goals can also be broken down and managed in smaller pieces. They make it easier to create an action plan or identify the steps required to achieve your goal. You can track your progress, revise your plan, and celebrate each small achievement. For example, instead of aiming to increase revenue, you can set out to increase revenue by 30% in the next 12 months, and celebrate each 10% along the way.

3. Achievable

Goals that are achievable have a higher chance of being realized. While it is important to think big, and dream big, too often people set goals that are simply beyond their capabilities and wind up disappointed. Goals can stretch you, but they should always be feasible to maintain your motivation and commitment.

For example, if you want to complete your first triathlon but you've never run a mile in your life, you would be setting a goal that was beyond your current capabilities. If you decided instead to train for a five mile race in six months, you would be setting an achievable goal.

4. Relevant

Relevant – or realistic – goals are goals that have a logical place in your life or your overall business strategy. The goal's action plan can be reasonably integrated into your life, with a realistic amount of effort.

For example, if your goal is to train to climb to base camp at Mount Everest within one year and you're about to launch a start-up business, you may need to question the relevance of your goal in the context of your current commitments.

5. Timely

It is essential for every goal to be attached to a time-frame – otherwise it is merely a dream. Check in to make sure that your time-frame is realistic - not too short, or too long. This will keep you motivated and committed to your action plan, and allow you track your progress.

Autosuggestion + Visualization

Autosuggestion and visualization are two techniques that can assist you in achieving your goals. Some of the most well-known and successful people in the world use these techniques, and it is not coincidence that they are masters in their own fields of business and sport. A few of these people include:

- Michael Phelps (Olympic Swimmer)
- Andre Agassi (Tennis)
- Napoleon Hill (Author)

- Wayne Gretzky (Hockey)
- Bill Gates (Microsoft)

Of course, each of these people have a high degree of talent, ambition, intelligence and drive. However, to reach the top of their respective field, they have each used Autosuggestion and Visualization.

Autosuggestion

Autosuggestion is your internal dialogue; the constant stream of thoughts and comments that flows through your mind, and impacts what you think about yourself and how you perceive situations.

Since you were a small child, this self-talk has been influenced by your experiences and has programmed your mind to think and react in certain ways. The good news is that you can reprogram your mind and customize your self-talk any way you like. That is the power of Autosuggestion.

To begin practicing Autosuggestion, make sure you are relaxed and open to trying the technique; an ideal time is just before bed, or when you have some time to sit quietly. Then, repeat positive affirmations to yourself about the ideal outcome. Top sports and business people will often practice just before a big game or meeting.

Some examples of positive self-talk or autosuggestion include:

- I will lead my team to a victory tonight!
- I will be relaxed open to meeting new people at the party tonight!
- I will deliver a clear and impacting speech!

- I will stop worrying and tackle this problem tomorrow!
- I will stand up for my own ideas in the meeting!
- I will remember everything I have studied for the test tomorrow!

Visualization

Visualization is a practice complementary to Autosuggestion. While you can repeat affirmations to yourself over and over, combining this practice with visualization is twice as powerful.

Visualization is exactly what it sounds like: repeatedly visualizing how something is going to happen in your mind's eye. Nearly everyone in sports practices this technique. It has been proven to enhance performance better than practice alone.

This technique can easily be applied to your business. For example, prior to any presentation or meeting where you must speak, present or "perform." You can also visualize yourself being incredibly productive and effective in your office. Or, having a discussion with your spouse calmly and rationally.

Elements to think about during visualization:

- What does the room look like?
- What do the people in the room look like?
- What is their mood? How do they receive me?
- What image do I project?
- How do I look?
- How do I behave? What is my attitude?
- What is the outcome?

2

How to Profit through Time Management

Manage Time Like Money

Why did you get into business for yourself? Was it to be your own boss? Choose your own hours? Have more time with the family? Spend more time doing what you love? Chances are, you answered yes to all these questions.

These days, you probably wonder where the time went. Why you spent 12 hours at work and barely make a dent in your to-do list. We already know that time is a key resource for you and your business, but it's also a key resource in your life. Harnessing and leveraging time is the only way to enjoy life, and have a profitable business at the same time.

Most coaches and healers carefully manage their financial and personnel resources, and pay due attention to their performance. Marketing plans and budgets are created, people are hired and teams are formed. What most business owners don't realize is that time – and the time of all team members – requires the same attention and diligent management.

Time will never manage itself. The decision to make a pro-active effort to manage your time must come from you. Once you have committed to taking ownership for your own time management, there are a host of tools available to you. But first, you must understand how much your time is actually worth, and where you are currently spending it.

What is Your Time Worth?

Ever wonder what your time is actually worth? Here's a quick way to figure it out:

Target annual income	A.
Working days in a year	B. 235
Working hours in a day	C. 7
Working hours in a year	D. 1,645
A ÷ D = YOUR HOURLY WORTH (before tax + expenses)	E.

This is a very simple calculation intended to put your time in perspective. In reality, no one is productive for each of the 1,645 hours. Various studies have put actual productivity at anywhere between 25 minutes and four hours per day. Either way, there's a lot of room for improvement.

Let's look at it another way:

Your age	A.
Days in a year	B.
Days spent on earth to date (A x B)	C.
Average life expectancy	D. 70
Total projected days on earth (D x B)	E.
Estimated days left (E – C)	F.

This exercise isn't intended to scare you, but bring your attention to the importance of choosing how you spend each hour you have available. It is a choice! By developing the skills required to manage your time, you will not only have a profitable business, but a rewarding and balanced life.

"The trouble is, you think you have time" - Buddha

The Five Culprits of Time Theft

Chances are – if you're like most people – you have no idea where your time goes. You're likely frustrated by the fact that you can spend 10, 12, even 14 hours a day working, and not make a dent in your to-do list, or only bill half of those hours.

When we're too busy and overloaded with work, we often switch into reactive mode. We can't make it to the bottom of the pile, and end up handling issues and making decisions at the last minute. One of the great benefits of choosing to become proactive in time management is that you can become proactive in all other areas of your business. When in proactive mode, you can take steps to grow your business through networking, building programs, and establishing systems.

Before you investigate where your time goes, let's take a look at the top five culprits of modern-day time theft:

1. Your Email

How many times a day do you check your email? Is Outlook or Mail constantly running on your desktop? Email – internal, external, personal and business – clogs up your day like no other communication channel. For many of us, it is possible to spend the entire day writing and responding to emails without even glancing at our inbox. The number of emails sent and received each day by the average person in 2007 was 147. Multiply that by an average of two minutes per message, and you have spent almost five hours on email in a single day.

2. Your Cell Phone

Cell phones have created convenience, security, and the luxury of telecommuting – but they don't call it a Smart Phone for nothing. PDAs and cell phones have also created a society that expects to be able to reach you at any moment, or at least receive instant responses to their calls. Your cell phone or PDA not only robs you of your time during the day, but also during the time when you are with your family of loved ones.

3. Your Open Door Policy

If you make it easy for your staff and clients to interrupt you, they will. Too often, open-door policies are set up by human resource departments to create clear communication channels. Instead, they create a clog of employees lined up at your door seeking immediate answers to non-emergent issues (or in the case of us online freedompreneurs, clogging up our calendars.)

4. Meetings

How many times have you been to a meeting that was scheduled to be an hour, and ended up lasting three? How often do you attend unnecessary meetings? Or meetings that run off-topic? Meetings can be a huge source of wasted time – your valuable time. As an entrepreneur, your day may consist of back-to-back meetings, leaving only your evening hours to complete the tasks that should have been done during the day.

5. YOU!

Every person has daily habits that sabotage their ability to work productively and efficiently. Many entrepreneurs and business owners can't separate business hours from leisure hours. Some get caught in a time warp while surfing the internet. Others - mainly overachievers – can become paralyzed by perfectionism or procrastination. Mainly we just don't have the tools to schedule and structure our time in a way that fits with our working style.

Where Does Your Time Go?

So far we've seen that time is a resource that should be as carefully managed as cash, we've figured out what your time is worth, and looked at the top five culprits of time theft. You've committed to taking steps to become a better time manager. What now?

Personal Time Management Research Exercise

The next step is to take a good (and honest!) look at how you spend your time. Once you understand your patterns and habits, you begin to implement the strategies in this chapter that will make you a better time manager.

Step One: Time Audit

Use the Time Log Worksheet at the back of this chapter to record how you spend your time for three working days in a row. Be honest, and be specific. Include time spent in transit, surfing the web, interacting with clients and colleagues, as well as how your time is spent at home in the evenings. The more information you can record, the easier it will be to analyze your time management skills in step two.

Step Two: Time Categorization

Once you have recorded your time for three days, sit down with all three sheets in front of you and identify the following using different colored markers or highlighters:

- Driving, public transportation or other travel
- Eating, including food preparation
- Personal Errands
- Exercise
- Watching TV
- Sleeping, including naps
- Using the computer, personal use only
- Being with family / friends
- Emailing, including checking, reading, and returning messages

- Talking on the phone, including checking and returning messages
- Internal meetings
- External meetings
- Administrative work
- Client work
- Non-client, non-administrative work

Step Two: Time Analysis

Now that you have identified how you have spent your time, go through the worksheets one more time and identify if you have spent enough, too much, or too little time on each main task.

Then, based on your observations, answer the following questions:

1. What patterns do you notice about how you spend your time during the day? (i.e., When are you most productive? Least productive? Most or least interrupted?)

_____

_____

_____

_____

_____

_____

_____

_____

_____

_____

2. Write down the four highest priorities in your life right now. Does your timesheet reflect these priorities?

_____
_____
_____
_____
_____

3. If you have more time, what would you do?

_____
_____
_____
_____
_____

4. If you had less time, what wouldn't you do?

_____
_____
_____
_____

5. Could you remove the items in question four and add the items in question three? Why or why not?

_____

_____

_____

_____

_____

6. Is procrastination a problem for you? How much?

_____

_____

_____

_____

Strategies for Profitable Time Management

There are many ways to curb time theft and refine your time management ability. Through a solid understanding of how you currently spend – and waste – time, you can determine which strategies you need to implement to correct unproductive behavior.

Here are 17 ways you can turn **less** of your time into **more** money:

1. Set Clear Priorities

The foundation of time management is a clear understanding of what your time is best spent on. Once you accept that you can't do everything, you need to decide what needs to be completed now, what can be completed later, and what someone else can complete. Each to-do list you create should be put through this filter, and reorganized so the highest priority items are on top, and the lowest priority items are less visible, or on the bottom.

Once you have established your priorities – which will also naturally reflect the priorities and goals of your business – stick to them. Just because someone else feels something is of a high priority doesn't mean it holds the same status next to your other tasks.

Prioritization is also helpful in your personal life and leisure time. Your spare time is precious – so make sure you are clear on how you would like to spend it.

2. Use Your Skills – Delegate Your Weaknesses

As a coach and healer, your day naturally consists of tasks you dislike doing. Some are essential – signing checks, reviewing financial statements, and other business maintenance – while others are simply not within your skill set.

If you are a strong public speaker, but struggle with report writing – delegate to a copywriter or editor. If you own a store or physical location and have no experience in design – outsource your signage. These freelance professionals often cost half as much as you, and take half as long to complete the task. Your time is saved for tasks that use and strengthen your skills effectively, your stress is managed, and ultimately a better product is produced.

3. Delegate, Delegate, Delegate

As a small business owner (which you must embrace you are), the only way you will ever get everything done is by delegating. Delegation is a vital skill that needs to be refined and practiced, and once mastered is the key to profitable time management.

Too often, coaches and healers believe that it will be "faster" or "more efficient" to complete the task themselves than to train and monitor someone else. Other times, there are no internal resources to download assignments to.

As a result, the following trends can be seen in many small practices:

- Owners are stressed and overworked, while teams are underutilized and under capacity.

- Team members are not given an opportunity to grow and develop in their roles, and may perceive a lack of trust or confidence in their ability. The mission loses good people.

- You as the leader are always in a reactive state, instead of a visionary or proactive state.

- Delegation happens at the very last minute, and team has little understanding of either the overall project or expectations for the task.

The easiest way to fix this problem is before it starts. Create a solid team around you who are well-trained and prepared to support the business and value the mission. Attract and retain qualified and quality people who can be cross-trained and promoted within the company. Ensure that communication flows throughout the business, so everyone has the product and service knowledge to step in and assist when necessary.

4. Learn to Say "No"

It's easy to fall into the habit of saying yes to everything. You are, after all the owner, right? No one can complete these tasks as well as you, right? You'll lose that customer if you don't help them with their garage sale, right?

Wrong. The most successful entrepreneurs have a keen understanding of how their time is best spent, and *delegate* the remaining responsibilities to trusted others. It's too easy to say yes to every request in the moment, and later feel overwhelmed when it's added to your to do list. You may not ruffle any feathers, but what toll does it take on your stress level? Your workload? Your time is valuable – so protect it!

Remember that if it is too challenging to say no immediately, you can always request some time to think about it. This way, you can evaluate your workload and realistically decide whether or not you can take on a new project. Then, stand by your decision, or assist in bringing in the necessary resources to get it done.

5. Create (and keep!) a Schedule

While multi-tasking is a desirable skill, it is also often a time thief. Attempting to do too many things at one time ensures that nothing gets done. As a mission based entrepreneur, you need to be able to focus and concentrate on essential projects without interruptions.

The only way to do this is to the commit to a strict schedule. Once you understand your work style and concentration patterns, you can allocate periods of the day to specific tasks. This includes personal and leisure time – schedules it and stick to it.

Schedule time for: list-creation + prioritization, email messages, telephone messages, internal meetings, client meetings, meeting preparation, "me-time", family time, recreation + fitness, daily business tasks, and blocks for focused work.

Remember that there is a training period involved in beginning a new routine – for yourself and those around you. Use your voicemail, out-of-office email message, and a closed door to begin to let people know when you will not be disturbed.

6. Make Decisions

The choice to not make a decision is a decision in itself. The most successful coaches and healers have the ability to make good decisions quickly and efficiently, and do not waste time deliberating over simple choices.

In leadership positions, often people are afraid of making the wrong decision or looking foolish if they make a mistake in front of team or clients. What they don't realize, is that hesitating or avoiding decision making impacts their leadership just as much or more than making the wrong decision. Not only can being indecisive be personally stressful, but it is also stressful for those around you whose tasks are waiting on your choices.

Remember, you must make the best decision with the information you have, in the time frame you have to make the decision. No one expects you to be a fortune teller – be decisive, make some mistakes, and learn from them.

7. Manage Telephone Interruptions

This is a huge source of time theft that can easily be managed and avoided. If you are available to take phone calls at any time of day, you are setting yourself up to take work home in the evenings. The phone will always ring when you are focused on an important task, and this is something can easily be avoided.

Figure out when you are most productive. Is it in the morning or the afternoon? Before, during, or after lunch? Once you have identified this time period, set your phone on "do not disturb" or have your calls directed to voicemail. If you do not have a receptionist, a variety of automatic answering systems are available for a nominal fee. To structure your phone time further, let callers know on your voicemail what specific time of day is best to reach you via phone. Then, set that time aside to receive and return phone calls.

8. Keep Your Work Environment Organized

Have you ever tried to make dinner in a messy kitchen? More of your time is spent looking for (and cleaning) dishes and tools than actually spent cooking the meal.

The same goes for your work environment. If your desk and office is in a constant state of chaos, then your mind will be too. In fact, some studies have revealed that the average leader spends nearly four weeks each year navigating through messy or cluttered desks, looking for lost information. Does that sound like productive time to you?

Once you make the initial clean sweep, it's easy to maintain order in the chaos:

- Tidy your desk at the beginning and end of each day. Attach pertinent documents to your to do list, or have clear and organized folders for loose papers.

- Organize your supplies drawer so you have easy access to stationery like pens, post-it notes, staplers and highlighters. Every minute counts!

- Only have the documents and files you are working on, on your desk. The rest should be neatly filed on a side table for later retrieval.

- Keep personal items (like photos or memorabilia) out of your primary line of vision. These can be distracting and encourage daydreaming. (I know you love your vision board, dedicate time to look at it then let it go and get to creating it)

As for your office or store, there are many ways to make its layout more conducive to effective time management. Try:

- Minimizing the distance between the reception desk and electronics like photocopies and fax machines.

- Keep a clear line of sight between your office and the most productive area of your business, so you are aware of what is happening amongst your team.

- Organize shelves and filling cabinets so files are not only easily accessed, but out of sight when not being used. Consider putting sliding doors or cabinets in storage areas, and remember that the floor is not a storage cabinet.

9. Keep Your Filing System Organized

If your data isn't organized properly, you will waste hundreds of hours searching for documents you need on a regular basis. This includes both electronic and hard copy files; they need to be organized and up to date.

Customer databases and enquiry records are worth their weight in gold. You can't afford to get behind when updating this information, or poorly store it for later retrieval. There are many easy to use software programs that will manage and organize customer databases for you; it doesn't need to be a time consuming or tedious exercise.

A simple way to manage information is to keep it in short, medium, and long term files for both hard and electronic copies. Create shortcuts on your desktop for folders or files you constantly access. Have short-term files available on your desk, medium-term files available within an arm's reach, and long-term files stored in cabinets.

10. Clearly Communicate – Never Assume

One of the biggest issues for time management in business – and likely the world – is miscommunication. This is a dangerous issue that can cripple any practice, including yours. Establishing and enforcing clear policies on things like accurate note taking, task assignments, and phone messages will ensure your team and clients understand the importance of clear and accurate communication.

The easiest habit to start to curb miscommunication is simple: write everything down. Carry a notepad (or use notes inside your smartphone), and jot down key points, figures, agreements and deadlines. Don't assume you'll remember later – you have at least a hundred other things to remember.

Some other simple strategies are:

- Return all communication promptly, including email, letters, faxes and phone calls (I Give myself a 48 rule for e-mails)

- Repeat back phone messages, phone numbers and other figures to confirm you recorded the information correctly.

- Record appointments in your phone or agenda the moment you make them. Otherwise, you will forget.

- Double check and confirm everything – addresses, phone numbers, meeting locations and times.
- Maintain accurate customer contact logs with dates, times, and phone numbers.

- Post checklists in your store or office for routine operations procedures.
- Announce any changes to the policies and procedures manual immediately. (Yes, you want to create P&P's for your practice)

11. Stop Duplicating Efforts

This is a key element of time management that is closely related to effective communication. Studies have continually shown that many businesses often duplicate and triplicate efforts that need only be completed once.

When you have clear systems and procedures in place, your staff will not need to "reinvent the wheel" each time the task needs to be completed. Meeting minutes and individual task assignments will ensure everyone is on the same page and understands their personal responsibilities.

Simple examples of this include re-reading your to-do list each hour to determine what the next important item is. If your list is already structured by priority, this is a needless task. If two team members are working on similar projects, but unaware of the other, the work will not only be inconsistent, but the efforts will be duplicated. These are easy problems to fix once they have been identified and communicated.

12. Say Goodbye to Procrastination + Perfectionism

Procrastination is something we all face at one time or another – and likely have since our school days. However, given the pace that the world operates at today, you will only fall behind the world, if you allow procrastination to rule your day. So how you do avoid it? It's simple. Stop, and just get started, no matter how boring, tedious, or painful the project may be. Reward yourself by crossing each step off your to-do list.

Many coaches and healers also fall victim to perfectionism, which can be paralyzing. The fear that there isn't enough time or resources to "get it perfect" will sometimes stop you dead in your tracks. Perfectionism can also hinder your ability to delegate and say no to tasks you believe no one else can complete "better". Do the best you can with the time and resources you have – and just get started.

13. Plan Your Work, Work Your Plan

Have you ever placed an advertisement on the fly because it was "cheaper", "faster", or "more urgent" than creating a marketing plan? Do you and your team have a clear idea of where your business is headed over the next six to 12 months, or five years?

Many studies show that less than 10% of small businesses have up to date marketing and business plans, as compared to the majority of large corporations and public companies, which have both.

Marketing and business plans take time and effort to create – but they work, and pay off in impact, income and lifestyle. They also save you time and money as compared to a haphazard or fly-by-the-seat-of-your-pants strategy. With a marketing plan in place, you will have an idea of how many ads you will be placing in a year, which will earn you a volume discount. Your marketing materials will complement each other, and deliver the same message to the same target audience. Designers will charge less for a package of collateral than for individual collateral items.

A business plan will provide you with a guide to reference when making decisions. You can repeatedly ask if the endeavor at hand will contribute to your overall vision, or just seems like a good idea or price.

Remember that planning includes both short and long-term time frames, and applies to both your daily to-do list, and your marketing budget. It provides you with a means to measure your progress, assists in identifying priorities, and helps to manage your time.

14. Avoid Needless, Impromptu + Unstructured Meetings

This may seem like a time theft issue that is out of your control, but it's not. You are in control of your own time, and through strict scheduling can establish a structure for internal and external meetings that everyone around you can work within.

Minimize impromptu internal meetings by letting your staff know when you're available for a "quick chat" and when you are not. If it is important, ask them to schedule a time to meet with you that works with both of your schedules. This not only saves you time, but encourages your team to find solutions to their own issues, and only approach you with more urgent or challenging matters.

You can't avoid having meetings, but you can avoid having unstructured meetings. Ask for or create an agenda for each meeting you attend, with a clear objective and an amount of time allocated to each item. This will keep your meetings focused and on task. If a meeting does run late, give yourself a reasonable buffer, and politely leave for your next appointment. You can always follow up with a colleague to catch-up on the pertinent items you may have missed.

15. Establish Clear Policies + Procedures

A clear policy and procedures manual is like a marketing or business plan – it takes time to create, but ultimately saves everyone in your company time, money and effort. A step-by-step guide to "the way we do things here" is an invaluable resource for your existing and new team, and provides clear expectations for how you like things done.

Too many businesses make up policies and procedures on the fly – creating dangerous scenarios where mistakes are made and expectations are not clear. Some items that should be included in a comprehensive policy and procedures manual include:

- Recruitment
- Customer relations
- Customer enquiries
- Customer complaints
- Returns
- Exchanges
- Late Payments
- Salary structure
- Bonus structure
- Team review
- Marketing Systems
- Internal Communication Systems

16. Keep the Right Set of Tools

The equipment your business needs to operate (and grow!) effectively should always be on hand, or easily contracted out. This is specific to each practice, and closely related to costs – including the cost of your time.

As coaches and healers, knowledge of the latest advancements in technology will increase your efficiency. It will help you stay on top of the new ways of creating leads and growth, maintain your position as an expert, and perhaps provide an easier way of getting things done.

Always ask yourself if these purchases are essential to your business –could perhaps make these purchases from a second hand dealer to minimize cost? Is it more cost effective to outsource or sub-contract the tasks to someone with access to this equipment, or to buy the equipment yourself?

If your business relies on tools and technology for daily tasks then obtaining the best quality you can afford is crucial. Think about the technology to manage social media, automate e-mails and manage your appointments.

17. Maintain Your Equipment

This may seem obvious, but you'll understand the importance if your laptop has ever crashed, or point of sale system has malfunctioned. Your practice can be slowed to a stand-still if your equipment is not in good working order. Of course there are instances that can't be predicted, but regular maintenance of your essential equipment will reduce these occurrences and help to anticipate when old equipment needs to be repaired or replaced.

Personal Time Management Strategy

Choose the top five tips from this chapter that you think will help you the most, given your personal time management research. Write them below, with three corresponding actions that you will start tomorrow. For example, if you are going to set a strict schedule, three actions might be to establish the schedule, communicate it to your team, and re-record your voicemail message.

1. _____

    a. _____

    b. _____

    c. _____

2. _____

    a. _____

    b. _____

    c. _____

3. _____

    a. _____

    b. _____

    c. _____

4. _____
   a. _____
   b. _____
   c. _____
5. _____
   a. _____
   b. _____
   c. _____

Timesheet | Day One

Timeslot	Activities	More/Less/ Enough time?
7:00 – 7:30		
7:30 – 8:00		
8:00 – 8:30		
8:30 – 9:00		
9:00 – 9:30		
10:00 – 10:30		
10:30 – 11:00		
11:00 – 11:30		
11:30 – 12:00		
12:00 – 12:30		
12:30 – 1:00		
1:00 – 1:30		
1:30 – 2:00		
2:00 – 2:30		
2:30 – 3:00		
3:00 – 3:30		
3:30 – 4:00		
4:00 – 4:30		
4:30 – 5:00		
5:00 – 5:30		
5:30 – 6:00		
6:00 – 10:00 (Evening)		

Timesheet | Day Two

Timeslot	Activities	More/Less/ Enough time?
7:00 – 7:30		
7:30 – 8:00		
8:00 – 8:30		
8:30 – 9:00		
9:00 – 9:30		
10:00 – 10:30		
10:30 – 11:00		
11:00 – 11:30		
11:30 – 12:00		
12:00 – 12:30		
12:30 – 1:00		
1:00 – 1:30		
1:30 – 2:00		
2:00 – 2:30		
2:30 – 3:00		
3:00 – 3:30		
3:30 – 4:00		
4:00 – 4:30		
4:30 – 5:00		
5:00 – 5:30		
5:30 – 6:00		
6:00 – 10:00 (Evening)		

Timesheet | Day Three

Timeslot	Activities	More/Less/ Enough time?
7:00 – 7:30		
7:30 – 8:00		
8:00 – 8:30		
8:30 – 9:00		
9:00 – 9:30		
10:00 – 10:30		
10:30 – 11:00		
11:00 – 11:30		
11:30 – 12:00		
12:00 – 12:30		
12:30 – 1:00		
1:00 – 1:30		
1:30 – 2:00		
2:00 – 2:30		
2:30 – 3:00		
3:00 – 3:30		
3:30 – 4:00		
4:00 – 4:30		
4:30 – 5:00		
5:00 – 5:30		
5:30 – 6:00		
6:00 – 10:00 (Evening)		

Daily To-Do List | Business

Task	Priority (1-10)	Deadline?	Delegation?

Weekly To-Do List | Personal (Family, Leisure, etc.)

Task	Priority (1-10)	Deadline?	Delegation?

3

Define Your Target Market

What is a Target Market?

Many Entrepreneurs can't answer the question: *Who is your target market?* They have often made the fatal assumption that *everyone* will want to purchase their product or service with the right marketing strategy.

A target market is simply the group of customers or clients who will purchase a specific product or service. This group of people all have something in common, often age, gender, hobbies, or location or belief systems.

Your target market, then, are the people who will buy your offering. This includes both existing and potential customers, all of whom are motivated to do one of three things:
- Fulfill a need
- Solve a problem
- Satisfy a desire

To build, maintain, and grow your business, you need to know who your customers are, what they do, what they like, and why they would buy your product or service. Getting this wrong – or not taking the time to get it right – will cost you time, money, and potentially the success of your business.

The Importance of Knowing Your Target Market

Knowledge and understanding of your target market is the keystone in the arch of your business. Without it, your product or service positioning, pricing, marketing strategy, and eventually, your business could very quickly fall apart.

If you don't intimately know your target market, you run the risk of making mistakes when it comes to establishing pricing, product mix, or service packages. Your marketing strategy will lack direction, and produce mediocre results at best. Even if your marketing message and unique selling proposition (USP) are clear, and your brochure is perfectly designed, it means nothing unless it arrives in the hands (or ears) of the right people.

Determining your target market takes time and careful diligence. While it often starts with a best guess, assumptions cannot be relied on and research is required to confirm original ideas. Your target market is not always your ideal market.

Once you build an understanding of who your target market is, keep up with your market research. Having your finger on the pulse of their motivations and drivers – which naturally change – will help you to anticipate needs or wants and evolve your business.

Types of Markets

Consumer

The Consumer Market includes those general consumers who buy products and services for personal use, or for use by family and friends. This is the market category you or I fall into when we're shopping for groceries or clothes, seeing a movie in the theatre, or going out for lunch. Retailers focus on this market category when marketing their goods or services.

Institutional

The Institutional Market serves society and provides products or services for the benefit of society. This includes hospitals, non-profit organizations, government organizations, schools and universities. Members of the Institutional Market purchase products to use in the provision of services to people in their care.

Business to Business (B2B)

The B2B Market is just what it seems to be: businesses that purchase the products and services of other business to run their operations. These purchases can include products that are used to manufacture other products (raw or technical), products that are needed for daily operations (such as office supplies), or services (such as accounting, automation, and legal).

Reseller

This market can also be called the "Intermediary Market" because it consists of businesses that act as channels for goods and services between other markets. Goods are purchased and sold for a profit – without any alterations. Members of this market include wholesalers, retailers, resellers, and distributors (think about affiliate marketers or joint venture partners).

Determining Your Target Market

Product / Service Investigation

The process for determining your target market starts by examining exactly what your offering is, and what the average customer's motivation for purchasing it is. Start by answering the following questions:

Does your offering meet a basic need?	
Does your offering serve a particular want?	
Does your offering fulfill a desire?	
What is the lifecycle of your product / service?	

What is the availability of your offering?	
What is the cost of the average customer's purchase?	
What is the lifecycle of your offering?	
How many times or how often will customers purchase your offering?	
Do you foresee any upcoming changes in your industry or region that may affect the sale of your offering (positive/negative)?	

Market Investigation

- **On the ground.** Spend some time on the ground researching who your target market might be. With your coaching and healing practice, hang out at seminars, workshops and online groups at different times of the day to get a sense of the people who live, work, and play in that space. Notice their age, gender, clothing, and any other indications of income and activities and pain points. Why are they there? What are they looking for? What problems do they have?

- **Learn from Others.** Who is also doing what you do and having success? Is there a small niche that is being missed? Observing the clientele of others can help to build understanding of your target market, regardless of whether it is the same or opposite. For example, if you attend a workshop of another coach, take note of who is there, do you resonate with the same people? Is that your tribe? You may find that you found your tribe our you may want to find another group that feels right to you.

- **Online.** Many cities and towns – or at least regions – have demographic information available online. Research the ages, incomes, occupations, and other key pieces of information about the people who live in the area you operate your practice. From this data, you will gain an understanding of the size of your total potential market.

- **With existing customers.** Talk to your existing customers through focus groups or surveys. This is a great way to gather demographic and behavioral information, as well as genuine feedback about product or service quality and other information that will be useful in a business or marketing strategy.

Who is Your Market?

Based on your product / service and market investigations, you will be able to piece together a basic picture of your target market, and some of their general characteristics. Record some notes here. At this point, you may wish to be as specific as possible, or maintain some generalities. You can further segment your market in the next section.

Consumer Target Market Framework

Market Type:	Consumer
Gender:	☐ Male ☐ Female
Age Range:	
Purchase Motivation:	☐ Meet a Need ☐ Serve a Want ☐ Fulfill a Desire
Activities:	
Income Range:	
Marital Status:	
Location:	☐ Neighborhood ☐ City ☐ Region ☐ Country
Other Notes:	

Institutional Target Market Framework

Market Type:	Institutional
Institution Type:	☐ Hospital ☐ Non-profit ☐ School ☐ University ☐ Charity ☐ Government ☐ Church
Purchase Motivation:	☐ Operational Need ☐ Client Want ☐ Client Desire
Purpose of Institution:	
Institution's Client Base:	
Size:	
Location:	☐ Neighborhood ☐ City ☐ Region ☐ Country
Other Notes:	

B2B Target Market Framework

Market Type:	Business to Business (B2B)
Company Size:	
Number of Employees:	
Purchase Motivation:	☐ Operations Need ☐ Strategy ☐ Functionality
Annual Revenue:	
Industry:	
Location(s):	
Purpose of Business:	
People, Culture & Values:	
Other Notes:	

Reseller Target Market Framework

Market Type:	Reseller
Industry:	
Client Base:	
Purchase Motivation:	☐ Operations Need ☐ Client Wants ☐ Functionality
Annual Revenue:	
Age:	
Location:	☐ Neighborhood ☐ City ☐ Region ☐ Country
Other Notes:	

Your Target Market: Putting It Together

Based on the information you gather from your product / service and market investigations, you should have a clear vision of your realistic target market. Here are a few examples of how this information is put together and conclusions are drawn:

Target Market Sample: Consumer Market

Business: Life Coaching Practice	**Business Purpose:** *Meet a need* (provide tools and strategies to living a more balanced lifestyle while maintaining business growth and focus) *Serve a want* (serving high end clients who have a six figure business and are finding out that happiness comes from more than money or material success)
Market Type: Consumer	
Gender: Women	
Marital Status: Married	
Market Observations: Online coaching practice that can serve people from all around the English speaking world. Unique strength in working with women in business who are feeling stressed out and over-whelmed.	**Industry Predictions:** As the world changes and becomes more conscious, many materially successful people are finding their attachments and driven behaviors are no longer serving them. As people search for more meaning in their life and a strong spiritual pull for freedom, there will be an increase in spiritual/life coaching needs.
Colleague Observations: Other coaches, who are playing in the same space, take a look at their websites, social media pages and opt in offerings. How are you different? What can you do that is unique to you?	**Online Research:** half of Any town's population is female, and 25% have children under the age of 15 years Any town's population is expected to increase by 32% within three years The average household income for Any town is $75,000 annually

TARGET MARKET: This coach's target market can be described as a successful business woman who is no longer satisfied in her business. She has a longing to find more happiness in her life and is willing to explore and learn techniques to creating happiness.

Example Marketing for this Target Market: Attn womenpreneurs: Is your Business No Longer Providing You Fulfillment? I Can Help… Learn 3 techniques To Achieving Happiness In Your Life! Download This Free Report!

Segmenting Your Market

Your market segments are the groups within your target market – broken down by a determinant in one of the following four categories:
- Demographics
- Psychographics
- Geographic's
- Behaviors

Segmenting your target market into several more specific groups allows you to further tailor your marketing campaign and more specifically position your product or service. You may wish to divide your ad campaign into four sections, and target four specific markets with messages that will most resonate with the audience.

For example, the life coach who is targeting womenpreneurs may choose to segment its target market by psychographics, or lifestyle. If the larger target market is *womenpreneurs with a six figure income*, it can be broken down into the following lifestyle segments:
- Fitness-oriented womenpreneurs
- Career-oriented womenpreneurs
- Spiritually included womenpreneurs

With these three categories, unique marketing messages can be created that speak to the hot-buttons of each segment. The more accurate and specific you can make communications with your target market, the greater impact you will have on your revenues.

Market Segmentation Variables

Demographic	Psychographic	Geographic	Behavioristic
Age Income Gender Generation Nationality Ethnicity Marital Status Family Size Occupation Religion Language Education Employment Type Housing Type Housing Ownership Political Affiliation	Personality Lifestyle Values Attitude Motivation Activities Interests	Region Country City Area Neighborhood Density Climate	Brand Loyalty Product Usage Purchase Frequency Profitability Readiness to Buy User Status

Understanding Your Target Market

Once you have determined who your market is, make a point of learning everything you can about them. You need to have a strong understanding of who they are, what they like, where they shop, why they buy, and how they spend their time. Remind yourself that you may *think* you know your market, but until you have verified the information, you'll be driving your marketing strategy blind.

Also be aware that markets change, just like people. Just because you knew your market when you started your business 10 years ago, doesn't mean you know it now. Regular market research is part of any successful business plan, and a great habit to start.

Types of Market Research

Surveys

The simplest way to gather information from your clients or target market is through a survey. You can craft a questionnaire full of questions about your product, service, market demographics, buyer motivations, and so on. Plus, anonymous surveys will produce the most accurate information since names are not attached to the results or specific comments.

Depending on the purpose—whether it is to gather demographic information, product or service feedback, or other data—there are a number of ways to administer a survey.

1. Telephone

Telephone surveys are a more time-consuming option, but have the benefit of live communication with your target market. Generally, it is best to have a third party conduct this type of survey to gather the most honest feedback. This is the method that market researchers use for polling, which is highly reliable.

2. Online

Online surveys are the easiest to administer yourself. There a many web-based services that quickly and easily allow to you custom create your survey, and send it to your email marketing list. These services can also analyze, summarize and interpret the results on your behalf. Keep in mind that the results include only those who are motivated to respond, which may slant your results.

3. Paper-based.

Paper surveys are seldom used, and can prove to be an inefficient method. Like online surveys, your results are based on the feedback of those who were motivated for one reason or another to respond. However, the time and effort involved in taking the survey, filing it out, and returning it to your place of business may deter people from participating.

Keep in mind that surveys can be complex to administer, and consume more time and resources than you have planned. If you have the budget, consider hiring a professional market research firm to lead or assist with the process. This will also ensure that the methodology is standard practice, and will garner the most accurate results.

Website Analysis

Tracking your website traffic is an excellent way to research your existing and potential customer's interests and behavior. From this information, you can ensure the design, structure and content of your website is catering to the people who use it – and the people you want to use it.

User-friendly website traffic analytics programs can easily show you who is visiting your site, where they are from, and what pages of your site they are viewing. Services like Google Analytics can tell you what page they arrive at, where they click to, how much time they spend on each page, and on which page they leave the site.

This is powerful (and free!) information to have in your market research, and easy to monitor monthly or weekly, depending on the needs of your practice.

Customer Purchase Data (Consumer Behavior)

If you do not have the budget to conduct your own professional market research, you can use existing resources on consumer behavior. While this data may not be specific to your region or city, general consumer research is actual data that can be helpful in confirming assumptions you may have made about your target market.

Your customer loyalty program or Point of Sale system may also be of help in tracking customer purchases and identifying trends in purchase behavior. If you can track who is buying, what they're buying and how often they're buying, you'll have an arsenal of powerful insight into your existing client base.

Focus Groups

Focus groups look at the psychographic and behavioristic aspects of your target market. Groups of six to 12 people are gathered and asked general and specific questions about their purchase motivations and behaviors. These questions could relate to your business in particular, or to the general industry.

Focus group sessions can also be time consuming to organize and facilitate, so consider hiring the services of a professional market research firm. You may also receive more honest information if a third party is asking the questions, and receiving the responses from focus group participants.

For cost savings, consider partnering with an associate in the same industry, and who would benefit from the same market data.

PS: I have partnered with other coaches to hire assistants, outsource projects and share in profits to get things going when I couldn't afford it. To quote Anthony Robbins, "It is not your resources, it is your resourcefulness"

4

Creating a Powerful Offer

I'm not going to beat around the bush on this one:

Your offer is the granite foundation of your marketing campaign.

Get it right, and everything else will fall into place. Your headline will grab readers, your copy will sing, your ad layout will hardly matter, and you will have customers running to your door.

Get it wrong, and even the best looking, best-written campaign will sink like the Titanic.

A powerful offer is an irresistible offer. It's an offer that gets your audience frothing at the mouth and clamoring over each other all the way to your door. An offer that makes your readers pick up the phone and open their wallets.

Irresistible offers make your potential customers think, "I'd be crazy not to take him up on that," or "An offer like this doesn't come around very often." They instill a sense of emotion, of desire, and ultimately, urgency.

Make it easy for customers to purchase from you the first time, and spend your time keeping them coming back.

I'll say it again: **get it right, and everything else will fall into place.**

The Crux of Your Marketing Campaign

As you work your way through this program, you will find that nearly every chapter discusses the importance of a powerful offer as related to your marketing strategy or promotional campaign.

There's a reason for this. The powerful offer is more often than not the reason a customer will open their wallets. It is how you generate leads, and then convert them into loyal customers. The more dramatic, unbelievable, and valuable the offer is the more dramatic and unbelievable the response will be.

Many coaches and healers spend thousands of dollars on impressive marketing campaigns in glossy magazines and newspapers. They send massive e-mail campaigns on a regular basis; yet don't receive an impressive or massive response rate.

These coaches and healers do not yet understand that simply providing information on their company and the benefits of their product is not enough to get customers to act. There is no reason to pick up the phone or visit the store, *right now*.

Your powerful, irresistible offer can:

- Increase leads
- Drive traffic to your website or business
- Move old product
- Convert leads into customers
- Build your customer database

What Makes a Powerful Offer?

A powerful offer is one that makes the most people respond, and take action. It gets people running to spend money on your product or service.

Powerful offers nearly always have an element of *urgency* and of *scarcity*. They give your audience a reason to act immediately, instead of put it off until a later date.

Urgency relates to time. The offer is only available until a certain date, during a certain period of the day, or if you act within a few hours of seeing the ad. The customer needs to act now to take advantage of the offer.

Scarcity related to quantity. There are only a certain number of customers who will be able to take advantage of the offer. There may be a limited number of spaces, a limited number of products, or simply a limited number of people the business will provide the offer to. Again, this requires that customer acts immediately to reap the high value for low cost.

Powerful offers also:

Offer great value. Customers perceive the offer as having great value – more than a single product on its own, or the product at its regular price. It is clear that the offer takes the reader's needs and wants into consideration.

Make sense to the reader. They are simple and easy to understand if read quickly. Avoid percentages – use half off or 2 for 1 instead of 50% off. There are no "catches" or requirements; no fine print.

Seem logical. The offer doesn't come out of thin air. There is a logical reason behind it – a holiday, end of season, anniversary celebration, or new product. People can get suspicious of offers that seem "too good to be true" and have no apparent purpose.

Provide a premium. The offer provides something extra to the customer, like a free gift, or free product or service. They feel they are getting something extra for no extra cost. Premiums are perceived to have more value than discounts.

Remember that when your target market reads your offer, they will be asking the following questions:

1. What are you offering me?
2. What's in it for me?
3. What makes me sure I can believe you?
4. How much do I have to pay for it?

The Most Powerful Types of Offers

Decide what kind of offer will most effectively achieve your objectives. Are you trying to generate leads, convert customers, build a database, move old product off the shelves, or increase sales?

Consider what type of offer will be of most value to your ideal customers – what offer will make them act quickly.

Free Offer

This type of offer asks customers to act immediately in exchange for something free. This is a good strategy to use to build a customer database or mailing list. Offer a free consultation, free consumer report, or other item of low cost to you but of high perceived value.

You can also advertise the value of the item you are offering for free. For example, act now and you'll receive a free consultation, worth $75 dollars. This will dramatically increase your lead generation, and allow you to focus on conversion when the customer comes through the door or picks up the phone.

The Value Added Offer

Add additional services or products that cost you very little, and combine them with other items to increase their attractiveness. This increases the perception of value in the customer's mind, which will justify increasing the price of a product or service without incurring extra hard costs to your business.

Package Offer

Package your products or services together in a logical way to increase the perceived value as a whole. Discount the value of the package by a small margin, and position it as a "start-up kit" or "special package." By packaging goods of mixed values, you will be able to close more high-value sales. For example: including a free desk-jet printer with every computer purchase.

Premium Offer

Offer a bonus product or service with the purchase of another. This strategy will serve your bottom line much better than discounting. This includes 2 for 1 offers, offers that include free gifts, and in-store credit with purchases over a specific dollar amount.

Urgency Offer

As I mentioned above, offers that include an element of urgency enjoy a better response rate, as there is a reason for your customers to act immediately. Give the offer a deadline or limit the number of spots available.

Guarantee Offer

Offer to take the risk of making a purchase away from your customers. Guarantee the performance or results of your product or service, and offer to compensate the customer with their money back if they are not satisfied. This will help overcome any fear or reservations about your product, and make it more likely for your leads to become customers.

Create Your Powerful Offer

1. Pick a single product or service.

Focus on only one product or service – or one product or service *type* – at a time. This will keep your offer clear, simple, and easy to understand. This can be an area of your business you wish to grow, or old product that you need to move off the shelves.

2. Decide what you want your customers to do.

What are you looking to achieve from your offer? If it is to generate more leads, then you'll need your customer to contact you. If it is to quickly sell old product, you'll need your customer to come into the store (landing page) and buy it. Do you want them to visit your website? Sign up for your newsletter? How long do they have to act? Be clear about your call to action, and state it clearly in your offer.

3. Dream up the biggest, best offer.

First, think of the biggest, best things you could offer your customers – regardless of cost and ability. Don't limit yourself to a single type of offer, combine several types of offers to increase value. Offer a premium, plus a guarantee, with a package offer. Then take a look at what you've created, and make the necessary changes so it is realistic.

4. Run the numbers.

Finally, make sure the offer will leave you with some profit – or at least allow you to break even. You don't want to publish an outrageous offer that will generate a tremendous number of leads, but leave you broke. Remember that each customer has an acquisition cost, as well as a lifetime value. The amount of their first purchase may allow you to break even, but the amount of their subsequent purchases may make you a lovely profit.

5

Immediate Sales

If you're a coach, healer or any entrepreneur, you're also a salesperson.

You've had to sell the bank to get them to loan you your start-up capital. You've had to sell your team on why they should work for your mission. You've had to convince your business partner, spouse, and friends why your business idea is a good one.

Now you have to repeatedly sell your product or service to your customers.

The ability to sell effectively and efficiently is one every successful coach and healer has cultivated, and continues to develop. It can be a complicated and time consuming task; one that you will have to continually work on throughout your career in order to be – and stay – successful.

Fortunately, making sales is a step-by-step process that can be learned, customized, and continuously improved. There are a wide range of tools available to help and support your sales efforts.

You don't have to be the most outgoing, enthusiastic person to be successful at sales. You don't even have to be a good public speaker. All you need is an understanding of the basic sales process, and a genuine passion for what you are selling.

Sales 101

As I said before, making sales is a process. There are clear, step-by-step actions that can be taken and result in a sale.

The sales process varies according to the type of business, type of customers and type of product or service that is offered; however, the core steps are the same. Similarly, sales training varies from individual to individual, but the core skills and abilities remain the same.

Here is a basic seven-step process that you can follow, or fine tune to suit your unique products and services. Remember that each step is important, and builds on the step previous. It is essential to become adept at each step, instead of solely focusing on closing the sale.

1. Preparation

Make sure you have prepared for your meeting, presentation, or day on the sales floor (workshop/trade show/social media post). You have complete control of this part of the sales process, so it is important to do everything you can to set the stage for your success.

- Understand your product or service inside and out.

- Prepare all the necessary materials, and organize them neatly.
- Keep your place of business tidy and organized. Reface product on shelves or move offering around on your website.
- Ensure you appear how your audience will receive you
- Do some research on your potential client and brainstorm to find common ground.

2. Build a Relationship

The first few minutes you spend with a potential customer set the stage for the rest of your interaction. First impressions are everything. Your goal in the second step is to relax the customer and begin to develop a relationship with them. Establishing a real relationship with your customer will create trust.

- Make a great first impression: shake hands, make eye contact, and introduce yourself.
- Remain confident and professional, but also personable.
- Mirror their speech and behavior.
- Begin with general questions and small talk.
- Show interest in them and where they are at.
- Notice and comment on positives.
- Find some common ground on which to relate.

3. Discuss Needs + Wants

Once you have spent a few moments getting to know your prospect, start asking open-ended questions to discover some of their needs and wants.

If they have come to you on the sales floor, ask what brought them in the store. If you are meeting them to present your product or service, ask why they are interested in it, or what criteria they have in mind for that product or service.

- If you are making a sales presentation, ask for a few moments at the outset to outline the purpose of your visit, as well as how you have structured the presentation.
- Listen intently, and repeat back information you are not sure you understand.
- Ask open-ended questions to get them talking. The longer they talk the more insight they are providing you into their needs and purchase motivations.
- Ask clarifying questions about their responses.
- If you become sure the customer is going to buy your product or service, begin to ask questions specific to the offering. i.e., what size/color do you prefer?

4. Present the Solution

Once you have a solid understanding of what they are looking for, or what issue they are looking to resolve, you can begin to present the solution: your product or service.

- Explain how your product or service will solve their problem or meeting their needs. If several products apply, begin by presenting the mid-level product.

- Illustrate your points with anecdotes about other happy customers, or awards the product or service has earned.
- Use hypothetical examples featuring your customer. Encourage them to picture a scenario after their purchase.
- Begin by describing the benefits of the product, then follow up with features and advantages.
- Watch your customer's behavior as you speak, and ask further qualifying questions in response to body language and verbal comments.
- Give the customer an opportunity to ask you questions or provide feedback about each product or service after you have described or explained it.
- Ask closed-ended questions to gain agreement.

5. Overcome Objections

As you present the product or service, take note of potential objections by asking open-ended questions and monitoring body language. Expect that objections will arise and prepare for it. Consider brainstorming a list of all potential objections, and writing down your responses.

- Repeat the objection back to the customer to ensure you understand them correctly.
- Empathize with what they have said, and then provide a response that overcomes the objection.
- Confirm that the answer you have provided has overcome their objection by repeating yourself.

The Eight Most Common Objections
The product or service does not seem valuable to me. There is no reason for me to act now. I will wait. It's safest not to make a decision right away. There is not enough money for the purchase. The competition offer a better service. There are internal issues between people or departments. The relationship with the decision maker is strained. There is an existing relationship with another brand

6. Close

This is an important part of the sales process that should be handled delicately. Deciding when to close is a judgment call that must be made in the moment during the sale. Ideally, you have presented a solution to their problem, overcome objections, and have the customer in a place where they are ready to buy.

Here are some questions to ask yourself before you close the sale:

- Does my prospect agree that there is value in my product or service?
- Does my prospect understand the features and benefits of the product or service?
- Are there any remaining objections that must be handled?
- What other factors could influence my prospect's decision to buy?
- Have I minimized the risk involved in the purchase, and provided some level of urgency?

Once you have determined it is time to make the sale, here are some sample statements you can use to get the process rolling:

- So, are we ready get started?
- Shall I grab a new one from the back?
- If you just give me your credit card, I can take care of the transaction and get you started.
- When would you like the product delivered?
- We can begin next month if we receive payment by the end of the week.
- Can I email you a draft contract tomorrow?

7. Service + Follow-up

Once you have made the sale, your work is not over. You want to ensure that that customer will become a loyal, repeat customer, and that they will refer their friends to your business.

Ask them to be in your customer database, and keep in touch through regular newsletters. Follow up with a phone call or drop by to ask how they are enjoying the product or service, and if they have any further questions or needs you can assist them with.

This contact opportunity will also allow you to ask for a referral, or an up sell. At the very least, it will ensure you are continuing to foster and build a relationship with the client.

Up selling

Up selling is simply inviting your customers to spend more money in your business by purchasing additional products or services. This could include more of the same product, complementary products, or impulse items. (Incense, Oils, Prayer Beads or an Additional Program)

Regardless, up selling is an effective way to increase profits and create loyal clients – without spending any money to acquire the business. These clients are already purchasing from you – which means they perceive value in what you have to offer – so take the information you have gained in the sales process and offer them a little bit more.

You experience up selling on a daily basis. From "do you want fries with that?" to "have you heard about our product protect program?" companies across the globe have tapped into and trained their staff on the value of the up sell.

Up selling is truly rooted in good customer service. If your client purchases a new computer printer, you'll need to make sure they have the cords required to connect it to the computer, regular and photo paper, and color and black and white ink.

If you don't suggest these items, they may arrive home and realize they do not have all the materials needed to use the product. They may choose to purchase those materials somewhere closer, cheaper, or more helpful.

Customer education is another form of up selling. What if your customer doesn't realize that you sell a variety of products, programs or different packaged solutions for their problem? Take every opportunity to educate your customer on the products and services you offer that may be of interest to them.

An effective way of implementing an up sell system into your business is simply by creating add-on checklists for the products or services you offer. Each item has a list of related items that your customer may need. This will encourage you and your team to develop the habit of asking for the up sell.

Other up sell strategies can be implemented:

- **At the point of sale**. This is a great place for impulse items like prayer beads, books, additional programs or a retreat.

- **In a newsletter**. This is an effective strategy for customer education.

- **In your merchandising**. Place strips of impulse items near related items. For example, on your website have a journal next to your program offering.

- **Over the phone**. If someone is placing an order for delivery, offer additional items in the same shipment for convenience.

- **With new products**. Feature each new product or service that you offer prominently in your practice, and ask your team to mention it to every customer.

Sales Team

Employing a team of strong salespeople

What Makes a Good Salesperson?

There are a lot of salespeople out there – but what qualities and skills make a great salesperson? These are the attributes you will want to find or develop in your team:

- Willingness to continuously learn and improve sales skills
- Sincerity in relating to customers and providing solutions to their objectives
- An understanding of the company's big picture
- A communication style that is direct, polite, and professional
- Honesty and respect for other team members, customers, as well as the competition.
- Ability to manage time
- Enthusiastic
- Inquisitive
- A great listener
- Ability to quickly interpret, analyze, and respond to information during the sales process
- Ability to connect and develop relationships of trust with potential clients
- Professional appearance

Team Building – Keeping Your Team Together

In many businesses, sales is a department or a whole team of people who work together to generate leads and convert customers. Effective management of your sales team is a skill every business owner should cultivate.

Teambuilding, recruitment, and training will be discussed in later sections, but take some time to consider the following aspects of managing a sales team:

Communication
- Are targets and results regularly reviewed?
- Are opportunities for input regularly provided?
- Do sales staff members have a clear understanding of what is expected?
- Do all staff members know daily, weekly, and quarterly targets?

Performance Management
- Are sales staff members motivated to reach targets?
- Are sales staff recognized and rewarded once those targets are reached?
- Are there opportunities for skills training and development?
- Do staff members have broad and comprehensive product or industry knowledge?
- Is there opportunity for growth within the company?
- Is performance regularly reviewed?

Operations
- Do you have a solid understanding of your sales numbers (revenue, profit, margins)?
- Are your sales processes regularly reviewed?
- Do you have a variety of sales scripts prepared?
- Do you measure conversion rates?
- How are your leads generated?

Sales Tools

Every salesperson should have an arsenal of tools on hand to assist them in the sales process. These tools can act as aids while a sale is taking place, or help to foster continual learning and development of the salesperson's skills and approach.

The list below includes some popular sales tools. Add to this list with other resources that are specific to your business or industry.

Tool	Description + Benefit
Scripts	Used for incoming and outgoing telemarketing, cold calls, door-to-door sales, in-store sales Create several different scripts throughout your business Maintains consistency in your sales approach Revise and renew your scripts regularly
Presentation Materials	High-quality information about your product or service Forms: PowerPoint presentation, brochure, product sheets, proposal Serves as an outline of your sales presentation, and keeps you on task
Colleagues	A source of help and advice, especially when you are on the same team or sell similar products Also a source of support
Customer Databases	An accurate, up-to-date database of customer contact information and contact history Used to stay in touch with clients Can also be used for direct mail and follow-up telemarketing
The Internet	A powerful resource for sales help and advice Information to help improve your sales process Online sales coaching Source for product knowledge
Ongoing Training	Constant improvement of your sales skills Constant increase in product knowledge Investment in yourself and your company

8 Tips for Better Sales

- **Dress for the sale.** Dress professionally, appear well put together and maintain good hygiene. Ensure you are not only dressed professionally, but *appropriately*. Would your client feel more comfortable if you wore a suit, or jeans and blazer?

- **Speak their language.** Show you understand their industry or culture, and use phrases your customer understands. This may require researching industry jargon or common phrases. Remember to avoid using words and phrases that are used in the sales process: sold, contract, telemarketing, finance, interest, etc. Doing so will help break down the salesperson/customer barrier.

- **Ooze positivity**. Show up or answer the phone with a smile, and leave your personal or business issues behind. Be enthusiastic about what you have to offer, and how that offering will benefit your customer. Reflect this not only in your voice, but also in your body language.

- **Deliver a strong pitch or presentation**. Be confident and convincing. Leave self-doubt at the door, and walk in assuming the sale. Take time to explain complex concepts, and always connect what you're saying to your audience in a specific way.

- **Be a poster-child for good manners**. Accept any amenity you're offered, listen intently, don't interrupt, don't show up late, have a strong handshake, and give everyone you are speaking to equal attention.

- **Avoid sensitive subjects.** Politics, religion, swearing, sexual innuendos and racial comments are absolutely off-limits. So are negative comments about other customers or the competition.

- **Create a real relationship.** Icebreakers and small talk are not just to pass the time before your presentation. They are how relationships get established. Show genuine interest in everything your customer has to say. Ask questions about topics you know they are passionate. Speak person to person, not salesperson to customer. Remember everything.

- **Know more than you need to.** Impress clients with comprehensive knowledge – not only of your product or service – but also of the people who use that product or service, and industry trends. Being seen as an expert in order to build trust and respect.

6

Profiting from Internet Marketing

Is your business online? If not, it should be.

The internet is today's primary consumer research tool. If your business does not have an online presence, it is harder for customers to find and choose your business. With over 73% of North Americans online, it is no wonder that individuals and businesses in all industries are looking to the internet to enhance their marketing strategies.

Luckily, it has never been easier to establish and maintain a comprehensive online presence. Internet marketing, also referred to as online marketing, online advertising or e-marketing, is the fastest growing medium for marketing.

But it is not just company websites that users are viewing. Blogs, consumer reviews, and a variety of social media sites are growing rapidly in popularity and changing, daily it can seem.

The internet is a very powerful tool for businesses if used strategically and effectively. It can be a cost saving alternative to traditional marketing approaches, and may be the most effective way to communicate with your target consumer.

A major advantage of the internet is that you are always open. Users can access your business 24 hours a day, 7 days a week, and depending on your business and the purpose of the website, visitors can also purchase goods at any time.

Internet Marketing for Everyone

The internet is a great way to create product and brand awareness, develop relationships with consumers and share and exchange information. You can't afford not be taking advantage of online marketing opportunities because your industry leaders and colleague is likely already there.

Internet marketing can take on many different forms. By maintaining a website for your business, you are reaching out to a new consumer base. You can have full control over the messaging that users are receiving and has a global reach.

Internet marketing can be very cost effective. If you have a strong email database of your customers, an e-newsletter may be cheaper and more effective than post mail. You can deliver time sensitive materials immediately and can update your subscribers instantaneously.

Top 10 Websites (Globally)

1. Google.com
2. Facebook
3. Yahoo.com
4. You Tube
5. Bing.com
6. Wikipedia
7. Amazon
8. MSN.com
9. live.com
10. Ebay.com

You will notice that half of these websites are search engines. An increasing number of consumers are first researching products, services and companies online, whether it is to compare products, complete a sale, or look for a future employer. Most people in the 18-35 age groups obtain all of their information online—including news, weather, product research, etc. The remaining sites are interactive sites where users can upload information for social networking, or information sharing.

Internet Marketing Strategies

Internet marketing – like all other elements of your marketing campaign – needs to have clear goals and objectives. Creating brand and product awareness will not happen overnight so it is important to budget accordingly, ensuring there is money set aside for maintenance of the website and analytics.

Be flexible with ideas and options—do your research first, try out different options, then test and measure the results. Metrics and evaluations can be updated almost immediately and should be monitored regularly. By keeping an eye out for what online marketing strategies are working and which are not, it will be easier to create a balanced portfolio of marketing techniques. You might find that in certain geographical areas, certain marketing strategies are more effective than others.

This list is by no means the full extent of options available for marketing online, but it is a good place to start when deciding which options are best suited to your company.

Create a website

The primary use for the internet is information seeking, so you should provide consumers with information about your company first hand. You have more control over your branding and messaging and can also collect visitor information to determine what types of internet users are accessing your website.

Search Engine Optimization

Since search engines comprise 50% of the most visited sites globally, you can go through your website to make it more search engine friendly with the aim to increase your organic search listing. An organic search listing refers to listings in search engine results that appear in order or relevance to the entered search terms.

You may wish to repeat key words multiple times throughout your website and write the copy on your site not only with the end reader in mind, but also search engines.

Remember when you design your website that any text that appears in Flash format is not recognized by search engines. If your entire website is built on a Flash platform, then you will have a poor organic search listing.

Price Per Click Advertising

If you find that visitors access your website after searching for it first on a search engine, then it may be beneficial to advertise on these websites and bid on keywords associated with your company.

These advertisements will appear at the top of the page or along the left side of the search results on a search engine. You can have control over the specific geographic area you wish to target, set a monthly budget and have the option on only being charged when a user clicks on your link.

Online Directories

Listing your business in an online directory can be an inexpensive and effective online marketing strategy.

However, you need to be able to distinguish your company from the plethora of competitors that may exist. Likely, you will need to complement this strategy with other brand awareness campaigns.

Online Ads (i.e. banner ads on other websites)

These advertisements can have positive or negative effects based on the reputation and consumer perception of the website on which you are advertising. These ads should be treated similar to print ads you may place in local newspapers or other publications.

Online Videos

With the popularity of sites such as You Tube, it is evident that people love researching online and being able to find video clips of the information they are seeking. Depending on your small business, you may want to upload informational videos or tutorials about your products or services.

Blogging

Blogging can be a fun and interactive way to communicate with users. A blog is traditionally a website maintained by an individual user that has regular entries, similar to a diary. These entries can be commentary, descriptions of events, pictures, videos, and more. Companies can use blogging as a way to keep users updated on current information and allow them to post comments on your blog. If blogging is something you wish to invest in, make sure that it is regularly updated and monitored.

Top 10 Mistakes to Avoid

Failure to measure ROI

Which metrics are you using? Are your visitors actually motivated to purchase or sign up? If the benefits of your online campaign are not greater than the costs incurred, then you may wish to re-evaluate your strategy.

Poor Web Design

This can leave a poor impression of your company on the visitor. A poor design could result in frustration on the visitors' part if they are not able to easily find what they went on your site to search for and also does not build trust. If consumers do not trust your company or your website, you will not be able to complete the sale and develop a longer relationship with that customer. You also need to include privacy protection and security when building trust.

This also includes ensuring all information on the website is current and having customer service available if users are experiencing difficulty or cannot find the information they are seeking. This could be as simple as providing a 'Contact Us' email or phone number for support.

Becoming locked into an advertising strategy early

Remember your marketing mix when creating a marketing strategy and avoid putting all of your eggs in one basket. Online marketing is a very valuable tool, but depending on your business and your target markets, other marketing campaigns may be the best option for you. Especially if this is your first time making a significant investment into your online sector, you want to remain flexible and able to adapt your strategy based off feedback received by researching and analyzing different options.

Acting without researching

Similar to becoming locked into an advertising strategy early, this mistake implies not dutifully testing and researching different online marketing options. For example, if your target consumer is aged 65+ and you are spending all of your marketing efforts into creating a blogging website (where the average ages of bloggers are 18-35), then you are likely not going to have a successful campaign.

Assuming more visitors means more sales

You have to go back to your original goals and the purpose of your company. More visitors may not mean more sales if your website is used primarily for information and consumers purchase their products elsewhere. This is also vice versa. You could have an increase in sales without an increase in unique visitors if your current consumer base is very loyal and willing to spend lots of money.

Often people will collect information online about products they wish to purchase because it is easier to compare options, but they purchase in person. Even though shopping online is becoming quite popular, people still prefer to see and feel the physical product before purchasing.

Failing to follow up with customers that purchase

Return sales can account for up to 60% of total revenue. It's no wonder that organizations are always trying to maintain loyal customers and may have customer relationship management systems in place. It is easier to get a happy customer to purchase again than it is to get a new customer to purchase once.

Not incorporating online marketing into the business plan

By ensuring that your online marketing plan is fully integrated and accurately represents your organization's overall goals and objectives, the business plan will be more comprehensive and encompassing.

Trying to discover your own best practices

It is very beneficial to use trial and error to determine the best online strategy for your company, but do not be afraid to do your research and learn from what others have already figured out. There will be many cases where someone was in a very similar position as you and they may have some suggestions and secrets that they wish to share. Researching in advance can save a great deal of time and money.

Spending too much too fast

Although it may be cheaper than traditional marketing approaches, internet marketing does have its costs. You have to consider the software and hardware designs, maintenance, distribution, supply chain management, and the time that will be required. You don't want to spend your entire marketing budget all at once.

Getting distracted by metrics that are not relevant

As discussed in the following section, there are endless reports and measurable's that you can analyze to determine the effectiveness of your campaign. You will need to establish which measurables are actually relevant to your marketing.

Testing and Measuring Online

As with any element of your marketing campaign, you will need to track your results and measure them against your investment. Otherwise, how will you know if your online marketing is successful?

These results - or metrics – need to be recorded and analyzed as to how they impact your overall return on investment.

Some examples of metrics are:

- New account setups
- Conversion rates
- Page stickiness
- Contact us form completion

Due to the popularity in online marketing and the importance of having a strong web presence, companies have demanded more sophisticated tracking tools and metrics for their online activities. It can be very difficult to not only know what to measure, but also HOW to measure.

Thankfully, it is easier than ever to get the information you need with the many types of software and services available, including Google Analytics, which are free and relatively accurate.

8 Metrics to Track

The following are the key measurables to watch for when testing and measuring your internet marketing efforts:

Conversions

How many leads has your online presence generated, and of those leads, how many were turned into sales? Ultimately, your campaign needs to have a positive impact on your business.

Regardless of the specific purpose of the campaign – from lead generation and service sign-up, to blog entries – you need to know how many customers are taking the desired action in response to your efforts. Your tracking tool will be able to provide you with this information

Spend

If you are not making a profit – or at least breaking even – from your internet marketing efforts, then you need to change your strategy. Redistribute your financial resources and reconsider your motives and objectives for your online campaign.

An easy way to do this analysis is to divide your total spend by conversions. This could also be broken down by product. You could also use tracking tool and view reports on the 'per visit value of every click,' from every type of source. Your sources can include organic/search engine referrals, direct visit (i.e. person typed your web address into their address bar), or email/newsletter.

Attention

You need to keep a close eye on how much attention you are getting on your website. One of the best ways to analyze this would be to compare unique visitors to page views per visit to time on site. How many people are visiting, how many pages they are viewing, what pages they are viewing, and how much time they are spending on the site.

A unique visitor is any one person who visits the website in a given amount of time. For example, if Evelyn visits her online banking website daily for an entire month, over that one month period, she is considered to be one unique visitor (not 30 visitors).

You may also want to incorporate referring source as well – the places online that refer customers to your website. You'll be able to determine what referring sources offer the 'best' visitors.

Top Referrals

Know who is doing the best job of referring clients to your website – and note how they are doing this. Is it the prominence of the link? Positioning? Reputation of the referring company?

Understanding where the majority of your visitors are coming from will allow you focus on those types of sources when you increase your referral sites. They also allow you to gain a better understanding of your online market – and target audience.

Bounce Rate

The bounce rate is the number of people who visit the homepage of your website, but do not visit other pages. If you have a high bounce rate, you either have all the necessary information on your homepage, or you are not giving your customers a reason to click further.

In Google Analytics, view the 'content' or 'pages' report and view the column stating bounce rate.

Errors

It is very important to track the errors that visitors receive while trying to access or view your website. For example, if someone links to your website, but makes a spelling error in typing the link, your users will see an error page in their browser, and will not ultimately make it to your website.

You can also receive reports on errors that customer's make when trying to type in your website address in their browser. You may wish to buy the domains with common spelling mistakes, and link those addresses to your true homepage. This will increase overall traffic and potential conversions.

Onsite Search Terms

If you have a 'search website' function on your website, it is useful to monitor which terms users are most frequently searching. This can provide valuable insight into the user friendliness of your site and your website's navigation system. This information will be included in the traffic reporting tool.

Bailout Rates

If you provide users with the option to purchase something on your website (i.e. shopping cart), then you can track where along the purchasing process people decided not to go through with the sale.

This could be at the first step of receiving the order summary and total, or further when stating shipping options. By obtaining this information, a company can reorganize or revamp their website to make the sales process more fluid and possibly encourage more purchases.

Here are the three main questions you should be asking yourself when evaluating your website presence:

- Who visits my website?
- Where do visitors come from?
- Which pages are viewed?

7

Copywriting for Profits

When it comes to marketing, we all know that *what* you say is just as important as *how* you say it.

In fact, I would argue that how you say something is even more important than what you have to say.

Think about it. The whole purpose of communicating is to get a message to its intended audience. In business, this means telling your target market why they should buy your product or service, and why they should buy it from you.

You could have the best, most irresistible offer out there, but if you can't get your audience to pay attention to your ad, it's worthless. You may offer the solution to their biggest frustration, but if you can't get them to read beyond your headline, it means nothing.

Effective copywriting gets your message to your target audience and then leads them to act. **Effective copywriting gets you the sale.**

Good Copy, Bad Copy

There are a number of misconceptions out there when it comes to copywriting for marketing collateral.

The first is that good copy must be clever (or witty, funny, dramatic, ironic, etc.). People get wrapped up in the idea that their ads need to compete with the ads on the pages of Vanity Fair – or the New York Times. They feel that their campaign needs to be littered with clever words that allude to the pop culture of the day, or position their company as "hip" or sophisticated.

This, in my experience, is rubbish.

The second assumption most business owners make is that good copy is the backbone of a successful ad or marketing campaign. I can't tell you how many good copywriters I've seen take the blame for a bad offer, or poorly positioned product.

The third misconception is that you need to be a good writer to write good copy. Or, if you're not a good writer, that you need to spend thousands of dollars on a copywriter for each of your marketing pieces.

That's rubbish, too.

So, then, what is good copy? And how do you write it?

The Purpose of Your Copy

Here are the key points you need to remember when crafting your advertisements:

a. A good headline *gets your readers to read the first sentence.*
b. A good first sentence *gets your readers to read the second sentence.*
c. And so on and on until the end of your marketing piece; or, the close of the sale.

Simple, isn't it?

The copy in your marketing materials is intended to persuade your audience to buy what you have to offer – one sentence at a time. Once you understand that copywriting is persuasive writing, not creative or technical writing, you will have much more success with your copywriting efforts.

Persuasive copy can be written in a number of ways – which we will discuss later in the section – but always includes:

- a compelling, shocking, or gripping headline
- a strong promise
- a heavy focus on benefits, not features
- proof to back up your claims

Compelling writing slowly builds a case, and leads the reader down a specific path to the final destination: the sale. The argument or message is built up over several sentences, or paragraphs, until the reader is primed and ready for the question.

For example, if you came right out in your headline and said, "Buy Tommy's Sprockets to Solve Your Problems", your highly skeptical audience would not give your ad a second glance. You've asked for the sale right up front, before building some trust and slowly persuading your readers.

However, if you took the time to build your case, the ad would read something like this:

DON'T BUY ANOTHER SPROCKET UNTIL YOU READ THIS

Did you know that the average sprocket is made with only 25% authentic materials? To speed up production and reduce costs, sprocket manufacturing over the last decade has begun to rely heavily on artificial materials.

Would you trust the safety of your family to a product that reduces quality to preserve profit?

At Tommy's Sprockets, we put the safety of your family first. Our sprockets are stronger and safer, because we still make them the old fashioned way – with 100% authentic materials and a lifetime guarantee.

Sure, they cost a little more than the average sprocket, but how much more would you pay for the safety of your family?

This ad isn't going to win any Pulitzer Prizes, but it doesn't need to. It engages the audience, communicates benefits, supports with features, and paints a compelling argument.

Headlines

Headlines are so crucial to the copywriting in your advertisement or sales letter that they deserve an entire section in this chapter.

Your headline is the first chance you have to make an impression on your target audience. Quite possibly, it is also your only chance. Without a headline that grabs your reader by the neck and focuses on what you have to say, the remainder of your ad is useless.

That's why even the greatest copywriters spend 50% of their time on the headline, and 50% on the rest of the copy.

With that in mind, it's important to note that your headline needs to do more than simply grab the attention of your potential readers. It also needs to tell them why they should care – your headline needs to send a full message that informs and encourages them to read onwards.

The most effective way to do this is to make an offer or promise to the reader that makes the time they invest in reading your ad worthwhile.

Seems like a lot for 8 to 10 words, doesn't it?

Headline Length

The general understanding when it comes to headline length is the shorter the better. But this comes from headline creation for newspapers and magazines, where space is crunched and nothing is up for sale.

In fact, based on studies done in the direct mail industry, 40% to 50% of the most effective headlines are more than eight words in length – meaning there are really no hard and fast rules for headline length.

Another marketing example of headline length is in sales letters. I'm sure you've seen headlines in sales letters that actually comprise small paragraphs. This is the opposite way of thinking from newspaper headlines, but in this medium it works.

The point is, if you need more than eight words to get your message across, then use more.

Headline Readers: The 80/20 Rule

According to readership statistics, eight out of 10 people read headlines, but only two of 10 will read the rest of the advertisement or letter. This proves the importance of crafting powerful, meaningful headlines. It also proves that an effective headline is the golden key to getting the rest of the piece read.

So, it would stand to reason that the better your headline, the higher the chances of improving the averages in these statistics.

Headline Types

Direct Headlines simply state the offer or proposition in as clear a manner as possible. *All winter clothing 30% off.*

News Headlines typically announce a new product or piece of information and mimic a headline you would read in a newspaper. *Johnny launches new line of improved sprockets.*

The Question Headline asks a question that the reader can relate to or would be compelled to read on to find the answer. *Do you want clearer skin?*

The 'How to' Headline tells the reader the body copy or product will explain step by step instructions for something of interest to the reader. *How to save $1,000 in energy costs this year.*

Command Headline is one of the strongest headline types, and commands the reader to do something. *Make your dreams come true today.*

The '7 Reasons Why' Headline tells the reader the body copy will include 7 (or another number less than seven) points that will either back up a claim or illustrate product benefits. *7 reasons why your teenagers won't listen to you.*

Testimonial Headlines leverages the power of outsider and expert opinion and quotes them directly in the headline. *"Tommy's sprockets have changed my life" says Brad Pitt.*

In summary, your headline should:

- Be immediately engaging
- Be useful and relevant to the reader
- Convey information
- Trigger an emotional reaction
- Include an offer
- Intrigue your audience

Strategies for Better Copywriting

Simplify, Simplify, Simplify

Good copy is written in clear, simple language with short sentence structure. It's conversational and reads like you are speaking to a friend or colleague.

Important points – like benefits – are listed in numbered or bullet format and traditional grammar is sacrificed for brevity.

Always read your copy before you finalize it and take out any unnecessary words. Find the shortest way to communicate the most information.

Be More Persuasive

Persuasion is an important technique for structuring your copy. While there is no clear formula for any type of copywriting, persuasive copy consistently includes the following elements:

- Has a reader focus from the very beginning
- Each paragraph or section supports the main argument
- Is highly specific and provides proof to support claims
- Includes credible proof like statistics and expert opinion
- Returns the focus to the reader as often as possible

Persuasive writing convinces the reader that they should believe what you say and do you what you say, and that there is something in it for them if they do. Again, there is no formula for this and no clear content rules, but there are some strategies you can use to make your writing more persuasive.

Repeat your point over and over

Repetition is a powerful and essential tool when crafting persuasive copy. It often will take several attempts at communicating before someone truly understands what you're saying. The benefit is that the more you say it, and the more ways you say it, the more likely your audience will believe it.

Of course, don't literally repeat yourself verbatim in your copy. Use a few different techniques to communicate the same point – for example, state it directly, tell a story, then repeat it again in your summary.

Give them reasons why

Backup your claims and requests with good reasons and leverage the power of the word 'because.' Studies have proven that even if the reason doesn't make any sense, or isn't directly related to the claim, people will be more likely to believe you simply based on the fact you backed up what you had to say.

Make comparisons to prove a point

Use the power of metaphors, analogies, and similes in your writing. This gives you an opportunity to relate the point you are trying to make directly to something the reader can relate to and understands to be true.

This is effective for making comparisons between like subjects, as well as unlike subjects, depending on the point you are trying to make.

Answer silent objections

Show that you understand the reader's point of view and thought process by answering questions you know they will be considering in their minds.

While you will not be able to address all potential objections in a single piece, or think of all potential objections your reader may raise, you can definitely dispute the most common arguments against what you are claiming.

Tell a story

Storytelling is an effective technique to use in all aspects of your copywriting. People relate to the experiences of others, and strive to learn from or compare themselves to the characters in the anecdotes. The story ends up doing the persuading for you.

Focus on Benefits

This is an obvious aspect of your messaging that you will feature in every piece you write, but it's not always easy to do well. Many writers end up featuring a slew of fake benefits instead of real ones.

Real benefits are things the reader actually cares about. For example, if you sold cough syrup you would want to explain how it eases the cold or flu symptoms, and not that it cures the illness. The symptoms are what are bothering the reader – that's what aspect of the product they care about and will make their purchase based on.

Make a Better Offer

Compel the reader to act with a stronger offer – one that they just can't possibly refuse. Make one that seems just believable enough to take action and reap the rewards.

A strong offer features a product or service with a high perceived value for a low cost. It could be a package of products offered for a lower price than the sum of the individual products, or a "free gift" with purchase.

Use Words that Work

Another misconception when it comes to copywriting is that it needs to be 100% unique. I'm not saying you should blatantly plagiarize others writers' work, but you should definitely pay attention to what works.

This includes how an ad is structured, how a point is made, or the hierarchy of the content. It also includes word choice. Certain words in marketing have been proven to have a stronger impact on general consumers than others.

There are tools that are easily available to you that will provide a list or database of effective words for use in advertising. Research online or invest in a software programs like Glyphus to use as a resource.

Offer a Guarantee

A guarantee is another technique that will compel a potential customer to take action. A strong guarantee takes the risk involved in purchase decisions away from the customer, and puts it on the seller.

Tell your customer that if your product or service doesn't deliver the performance or results you have promised, you'll give them their money back or compensate them in a way that will make it right.

8

How to Create Repeat Business and Have Clients that Pay, Stay and Refer

When it comes to marketing and generating more income, most business owners are focused outward.

They've carefully established and segmented their target market, and created specific offers and messages for each market segment. They spend thousands of dollars in advertising and direct mail campaigns in hot pursuit of more leads, more customers, and more foot traffic.

While this is an effective way to build a business, it is costly and time consuming. It requires constant and consistent effort, and while this approach does generate results, those results quickly disappear when the effort stops or becomes less intense.

Successful businesses that see sustained growth have a double-edged marketing strategy. They focus their efforts *outward* – on new potential customers and marketing – as well as *inward* – on existing customers and referral business.

These successful businesses have leveraged their existing efforts to generate more revenue. Simply put, their customers buy from them over and over again.

For most businesses, this is the easiest way to increase their revenues. Simple customer loyalty strategies and outstanding customer service are often all you need to dramatically increase your sales – from the customers you already have.

The Cost of Your Customers

Do you know how much it costs your business to buy new customers?

Each new customer that walks through your door – with the exception of referrals – has cost you money to acquire. You have spent money on advertising and promotions to generate leads and turn those leads into customers.

For example, if you have placed an ad in your local newspaper for $1,000, and the ad brings in 10 customers, you have paid $100 to acquire each customer. You would need to ensure each of those customers spent at least $200 to cover your margin and break even.

Alternately, if you spent two hours of your time and $10 per month on an email marketing program to send a newsletter to your existing database of customers, and you bring in 10 customers as a result – each customer has cost you $1.

Generating more repeat business means focusing on the marketing strategies that aim to keep your existing customers instead of purchase new ones – effectively reducing the cost of attracting new customers to your business.

These strategies are simple to implement, and don't require much time investment. Just a solid understanding of how to make customers want to come back and spend more of their money

Keeping Your Customers

Marketing strategies that focus on keeping your current customer base are easy and enjoyable to implement. They allow you to build real relationships with the people you do business with, instead of dealing with a revolving door of people on the other end of your sales process.

Repeat customers create a community of people around your business that presumably share the same needs, desires and frustrations. The information you gain from these customers (market research) can help you strengthen your understanding of your target audience, and more accurately segment it.

Remember – 80% of your revenue comes from 20% of your customers. Always focus on these customers. They are ideal customers that you want to recruit, and hold on to.

Customer Service: Make them love buying from you

Every business – even those with excellent service standards can improve the service they provide their customers. Customer service seems to be a dying concept in most businesses; more focus seems to be placed on the speed of the transaction. These days you can even go to the grocery store now and not speak to a single sales associate thanks to self-serve checkouts.

To improve your company's customer service standards, take a survey of your customers and your team to brainstorm ways you can improve the experience of buying from your business.

Successful customer service standards – those that make your customers *buy* – are:

Consistent. The standards are up kept by every person in your organization. Expectations are clear and followed through. Customers know what to expect, and choose your business because of those expectations.

Convenient. It is nearly effortless for the customer to spend money at your place of business. Convenience can take many forms – location, product selection, value-added services like delivery – and it is also consistent.

Customer-driven. The service the customer receives is exactly how they would like to be treated when buying your product or service. It is reflective of your target market, and appropriate to their lifestyle. Customers would probably not appreciate white linen tablecloths at a fast food restaurant, but they would appreciate a 2-minutes or less guarantee.

Newsletters: Keep in touch with your customers

A regular newsletter is an easy, time-effective, and inexpensive marketing strategy to implement. Unfortunately, many small businesses think these are too time consuming and too expensive to adopt as part of their marketing strategy.

The most popular type of newsletter distribution is email. This will cost your business as little at $10 per month for an email marketing service subscription, and can be customized to your unique branding.

Here is an easy five-step process to starting a company newsletter:

1. Pick your audience. New customers? Market segment? Existing customers?

2. Choose what you're going to say. Company news? Feature product? New offer?

3. Determine how you're going to say it. Articles? Bullet points? Pictures?

4. Decide how it's going to get to your audience. Email? Mail? In-store?

5. Track your results. How many people opened it? Read it? Took action?

Value Added Service: Give them happy surprises

Adding value to your business is an effective way of getting your customers back. Every person I know would choose a mattress store that offered free delivery over one that did not. It's that simple.

There are many ways to add value to your business, including:

o **Feature your expertise.** Use your knowledge to provide additional value to your customers. Offer a free consumer guide or report with every purchase.

o **Add convenience services.** Offer a service that makes their purchase easier, or more convenient. The best example of this is free shipping or delivery.

o **Package complementary services**. Packaging like items together creates an increase in perceived value. This is great for start-up kits.

o **Offer new products or services**. Feature top of the line or exclusive products, available only at your business. Offer a new service or profile a new staff member with niche expertise.

Value added services generate repeat customers in one of two ways:

1. Impress them on their first visit. Impress your customer with great service, a product that meets their needs, and then wow them with something extra that they weren't expecting. Get them to associate the experience of dealing with your business with happy surprises, and create a perception of higher value.

2. Entice them to come back. The introduction of a new value-added service can be enough to convince a customer to buy from you again. Their initial purchase established a trust and knowledge of your business and its processes. They will want to "be included" in anything new you have to offer – especially if there is exclusivity. It is easier to attract clients that have purchased from you than potential clients who have not.

Customer Loyalty Programs: Give them incentives

Another simple way to keep in touch with existing customers and keep them coming back to you is to create a customer loyalty program.

These programs do not have to be complicated or costly, and are relatively easy to maintain once they have been implemented. These programs help you gain more information on your customers and their purchasing habits.

Here are some examples of simple loyalty programs that you can implement:

Free product or service. Give them every 10th (or 6th) product or service free. Produce stamp cards with your logo and contact information on it.

Reward dollars. Give them a certain percentage of their purchase back in money that can only be spent in-store. Produce "funny money" with your logo and brand.

Rewards points. Give them a certain number of points for every dollar they spend. These points can be spent in-store, or on special items you bring in for points only.

Membership amenities. Give members access to VIP amenities that are not available to other customers. Produce member cards or give out member numbers.

Remember that in order for this strategy to work, you and your team have to understand and promote it. The program in itself becomes a product that you sell.

9

How to Use Testimonials and Profit from Social Proof

The Power of Testimonials

Testimonials are simply the single most powerful asset you can have in your marketing toolkit. When your customers tell others about the benefits of choosing your business, it is a thousand times more powerful than the same words from your mouth.

The words and opinions of others motivate people to spend money every day. From celebrity endorsements on TV and in magazines, to casual conversations with friends, decisions about what product or service to buy – and what brand or provider – are heavily influenced by those who have purchased before.

Why? There are several reasons. Many people have an inherent distrust of salespeople, and skepticism toward marketing materials. Others are bombarded with choice, and are looking for some sense of security in their purchase decision.

Testimonials build the credibility of your business, break down natural barriers, and create a sense of trust for the consumer. They have an incredible ability to persuade customers to buy, and to buy from you. Think about the last time someone recommended a brand of laundry detergent, a bottle of wine, or a plumber to you. Their positive experience had more of an impact on your decision to buy than any advertisement or discount.

When it comes to spending money, people want a sure bet. They want to know that someone else has bought before, and they want to know that the product or service has delivered the promised results. A testimonial for your business is worth more than any copywriter, clever ad slogan, or sales pitch.

Customers Who Give Testimonials

When people put their name and reputation on paper to endorse something, it creates a sense of loyalty; if questioned, they will back their decision, even if they find later their decision was wrong.

When someone is willing to endorse your product or service in writing, they have likely already started a word-of-mouth chain of verbal testimonials about their positive experience. Remember the last time you discovered a chiropractic miracle worker? Or the fastest and cheapest drycleaner? Didn't you tell every one of your friends who could use the service?

By asking a customer for a testimonial, you are asking for their assistance in the growth of your business. When they feel they are truly helping and participating in the development of your company, their sense of pride will mean continuous loyalty to your product or service.

11 Ways to Get Great Testimonials

Testimonials are powerful – no question. But how do you make sure that the quotes you get from your customers will bring you the most value? How do you ensure that your client will articulate your product's merits in a clear and easy to understand way? How do you make sure you can actually use their testimonials in your marketing materials?

Asking for testimonials requires more effort than merely soliciting general comments and praise. You want to ensure that your customer feels a sense of pride and loyalty in providing their opinion, and that their opinion will have an impact on potential buyers.

How? Glad you asked. Here are 11 proven ways to get great testimonials from your customers.

1. Don't wait!

Your customers are the happiest and most willing to help you within a day to a week of their purchase, so aim to secure the testimonial in this time period. Ask for the testimonial before they leave, and make sure you have all their contact details to follow up with. This also ensures you stay on top of your testimonial recruitment!

2. Get specific

Specific testimonials are more believable. The more specific you can have your customer be, the stronger and more impactful the testimonial will be. Remember the Sleep Country testimonials that referenced the little "booties" that their delivery men wore to keep carpets clean? Meaningful details get remembered. Ask for mention of things like time, dates, extraordinary customer service, and personal observations.

3. If you were the solution – what was the problem?

Testimonials that tell stories are more engaging. Ask the client to not only describe their experience with your company, but also the negative experience that led them to your door. If they can describe the struggles and challenges they were facing before receiving your service, the reader will likely be able to sympathize and resonate with similar struggles. This will motivate them to solve their problems with your solution.

4. Write the first draft

Make it easy for your clients. This technique is something you can offer someone who is hesitant to commit to writing a testimonial due to time constraints, or is procrastinating. Ask them to brainstorm a few notes they would like to include in their feedback, write them down, and string them into a concise testimonial for their review. All they have to do is review, print on their letterhead, sign, and mail back to you!

5. Include your marketing message or USP

Always ask your customers to include your unique selling proposition (USP) in the testimonial. For instance, if your USP includes exceptional customer service, same-day installation, and a money-back guarantee then ask your customer to attest to those qualities.

6. A picture says…

Yes, you know the saying. But it's true. When readers attach an image of the speaker to words, the words are enlivened and have twice as much validity and impact. When readers see an image of a previous client using your product or service, their words and opinions are even more believable. You can take these simple pictures yourself – and take many so you have a selection to choose from.

7. Credentials equal trust

As we mentioned, testimonials from credible sources will have the most believability and impact. When you ask for a testimonial, make sure your customer states their expertise and credentials. If you sell custom orthotics, and can secure a solid testimonial from a doctor, their words will be golden in your marketing materials.

8. Don't forget to ask permission

When you ask for testimonials, make sure you are clear that their words may be used in your marketing materials, including advertisements, website and in-store displays. This is a good time to thank them for their time and sincerity, and show your appreciation for their words.

9. Location, location…

Depending on the market reach of your business, the location of your customers is an important part of the believability of your testimonial. If you own a community-based business, when potential clients see you've made others happy just down their street they'll be motivated to use your service too. If you own a regional business, then the cities and addresses of other happy customers can help communicate the reach of your service.

10. Testimonials are not surveys

Keep the purpose of your request in mind when you're asking for testimonials. Testimonials should be positive fodder for your advertising materials. Surveys are used to solicit meaningful (and often confidential) customer information to refine and improve your service. Testimonials are public statements, while surveys are often anonymous and can produce less-than-positive results.

11. Say thank you!

Thanking a customer for their time and effort creating your testimonial is just plain good manners. It also increases loyalty and goodwill. This can be done via email, but sending a formal letter on your letterhead is a more meaningful approach.

Using Testimonials Strategically

So now you have a pile of glowing customer testimonials. What's next?

Choose the most powerful piece of the testimonial

What is the most convincing aspect of the testimonial? Is it the author? Where they are from? A specific sentence or paragraph they wrote? Be strategic about the aspect of the testimonial that you feature, and select what will have the most impact.

For example, you can compile a list titled *What Customers are Saying*, and list only the phrases that support your specific marketing message. Or you can feature the unique credentials or story of your customer, before you even include their testimonial. You can also summarize the testimonial with a powerful headline.

Put them on your website

Adding a page of testimonials to your website is a great start, especially when you're beginning to solicit customer responses. However, the most powerful way to ensure site visitors actually see your testimonials is to include them on every page – especially the ones with the highest traffic.

A testimonial should be placed wherever you make a strong statement about your service or product, and wherever the service or product is described. This is a great way to break up your sales copy with some "proof". As they read about your offering, your credibility will be validated by someone other than you.

Compile your best 25 to 50 letters in a display book

Like a proud grandparent, keep a book of testimonials in the waiting area of your office, your boardroom, and in your desk. Or, put one at the service counter, cash register and anywhere else people may have a moment to flip through.

I've seen this done in a recruiting firm, a hardware store, and a physiotherapist's office. When clients have a chance to read the positive experiences of others, they will be more open to hearing your sales pitch less guarded when responding to your unique offering.

Hang your favorite testimonials in your store or office

Testimonials as art! Frame your favorite testimonials – preferably the ones written on client letterhead – and post them on the wall in your business. Even if clients don't read them up close, the volume and visual recognition of client logos will have impact. Plus – your next satisfied clients will want to see their company names on the wall too.

Put them in your advertisements

Use short, clear, concise testimonials in your advertising. When was the last time you saw a prescription drug advertisement without a testimonial? Can't remember? That's because you haven't. The best advertisers know that testimonials are the fastest and most effective way to overcome skepticism and get clients thinking that your product or service is the solution to their problem.

Include a page of testimonials in your direct mail

When sending your marketing materials directly to a mass list of potential clients, let the words of others speak to the merits of your product or service. Put together a page or two of testimonials, and attach it to your mailing. The credibility of your company will be instantly established, encouraging clients to act – and buy – faster.

Partner with an associate for joint mailing

If you have an associate or colleague who has a similar customer base of new prospects for your business, try a joint-endorsed mailing. Each of you will send a letter to your own clients, endorsing the other's products and services. Your service or solution is offered to a potential client by a trusted source, and you are offering your existing clients the added value of an associate's service to complement your own.

Testimonial Request Letter

Here is an example of a basic testimonial request letter that can be customized and made into a template for your unique business. This can also be sent over email if that is how your clients prefer to be contacted.

Mr. John Smith
1234 Main Street
Anytown, Anyplace 90210

January 2, 2006

Dear Mr. Smith,

Thank you for visiting our store this week. It was a pleasure helping you select a new laptop for your daughter to use at university this fall – they just grow up too fast! Your research and clear idea of the product you were searching for truly made our job easy. We love the back to school season, because it means working with clients like yourself.

We know there are a lot of choices when it comes to purchasing a laptop in Anytown, so thank you for choosing ABC Company. If there is anything else we can assist you with, please don't hesitate to contact me directly.

We occasionally ask select customers for their feedback in the form of a testimonial. Because we are so proud of the feedback we receive, we often use our customer's quotes in our marketing materials – specifically our website and sales brochures. The real life experiences of our customers at ABC Company are stories that we are proud of.

Could I ask you to write down some of your feedback? A few words about your experience with ABC Company, and how we helped you and your daughter would be greatly appreciated. We encourage you to print this on your company letterhead, so we can provide your own company with some exposure as well.

You may want to include the names of the associates who helped you, and how your daughter is enjoying her laptop. Again, we would like to feature your name and experience in our marketing materials. For your convenience, I've included a prepaid envelope with which to mail your testimonial back to us.

Thank you very much for your assistance.

Kind regards,

Your name here

Testimonial Thank You Letter

Here is an example of a short thank you letter for a testimonial that can also be customized and made into a template for your unique business. You may wish to write your thank you letters on company note cards, but try to avoid sending these thank you's via email.

Mr. John Smith
1234 Main Street
Anytown, Anyplace 90210

January 10, 2006

Dear Mr. Smith,

We received your glowing testimonial in the mail today, and I wanted to thank you personally for your kind words. Your comments about our store and our people are important to us, and I will make sure my staff takes a moment to read your letter.

We are thrilled that your daughter is enjoying her laptop, and using it to keep in touch with you while she studies abroad. When we sold it to you, we truly believed it would provide the most long-lasting value for her student budget. I hope it serves her for the rest of her time at school.

Thank you again for taking the time to write us. We are all proud to have been of service to you and your daughter, and look forward to seeing you both again soon.

Warm regards,

Your Name Here

Testimonial Examples

Below you will find a series of sample testimonials, and excerpts from testimonial letters. Read these over, and take a moment to notice why each is a powerful statement. We have also summarized each testimonial with a headline.

24% Response Rate from a Single Direct Mailing!

We were skeptical about direct mail campaigns, and unsure about the return on investment. Your strategic advice and logistical help made the project run smoothly and easily – we received over 200 leads from this single effort!

John and Betty McFee
Scottsdale, AZ

Best Sleep in 20 Years!

I can't tell you how much I appreciated Craig's patience and assistance in my mattress selection. He is so knowledgeable of each mattress' design and features, and helped us find a financing solution that worked with our budget. I haven't slept this well in over two decades. Promote him!

Jason Carmichael

Gentle and effective approach

I have always been reluctant to visit a chiropractor for my lower back pain because I am not comfortable with physical adjustments. Sarah took the time to clearly explain the cause of my pain, and gave me easy exercises to help correct the problem. She respected my comfort level, and treated me without uncomfortable cracks and snaps!

Wally Orton

Testimonial Worksheet

Start today! Brainstorm a list of recent customers and clients who you will approach for testimonials. Post this worksheet in your office, and track your progress. Aim for 50 testimonials in two months. You can never have too many.

Name + Phone	Request Letter Sent	Follow Up Call Made	Testimonial Received	Thank-you Letter Sent
	☐	☐	☐	☐
	☐	☐	☐	☐
	☐	☐	☐	☐
	☐	☐	☐	☐
	☐	☐	☐	☐
	☐	☐	☐	☐
	☐	☐	☐	☐
	☐	☐	☐	☐
	☐	☐	☐	☐

	☐	☐	☐	☐
	☐	☐	☐	☐
	☐	☐	☐	☐
	☐	☐	☐	☐
	☐	☐	☐	☐
	☐	☐	☐	☐
	☐	☐	☐	☐
	☐	☐	☐	☐
	☐	☐	☐	☐

10

Systemizing Your Business and Developing Effective Processes

One of the biggest mistakes a business owner can make is to create a company that is dependent on the owner's involvement for the success of its daily operations. This is called working "in" your business. You're writing basic sales letters, licking stamps, and guiding staff step-by-step through each task.

There are a number of problems with this approach. One is redundancy. You're paying your staff to carry out tasks that you eventually complete. The second is poor time management. You're spending your day – at your high hourly rate – on tasks as they arise, leaving little room for the tasks you need to be focused on.

However, the biggest issue I have with this approach is that countless intelligent business owners, healers and coaches are spending the majority of their time operating their business, instead of *growing* it.

A good test of this is to ask yourself, what would happen if you took off to a hot sunny destination for three weeks and left your cell phone, PDA and laptop at home. Would your business be able to continue operating?

If you said no, then this chapter is for you.

Systemizing your business is about putting policies and procedures in place to make your business operations run smoother – and more importantly – without your constant involvement. With your newfound free time, **you will be able to focus your efforts on the bigger picture: strategically growing your business.**

Why Systemize?

For most small business owners, systems simply mean freedom from the day-to-day functioning of their organization. The company runs smoothly, makes a profit, and provides a high level of service – regardless of the owner's involvement.

Systemizing your business is also a healthy way to plan for the future. You're not going to be working forever – what happens when you retire? How will you transition your business to new ownership or management? How will you take that vacation you've been dreaming of?

Businesses that function without their ownership are also highly valuable to investors. Systemizing your business can position it in a favorable light for purchase, and merit a high price tag.

A system is any process, policy, or procedure that consistently achieves the same result, regardless of who is completing the task.

Any task that is performed in your business more than once can be systemized. Ideally, the tasks that are completed on a cyclical basis – daily, weekly, monthly, and quarterly – should be systemized so much so that anyone can perform them.

Systems can take many forms – from manuals and instruction sheets, to signs, banners, and audio or video recordings. They don't have to be elaborate or extensive, just provide enough information in step-by-step form to guide the person performing the task.

Benefits of Business Systems

There are unlimited benefits available to you and your business through systemization. The more systems you can successfully implement, the more benefits you'll see.

- Better cost management
- Improved time management
- Clearer expectations of staff
- More effective staff training and orientation
- Increased productivity (and potentially profits)
- Happier customers (consistent service)
- Maximized conversion rates
- Increased staff respect for your time

- Increased level of individual initiative
- Greater focus on long-term business growth

Taking Stock of Your Existing Systems

The first step in systemizing your business is taking a long look at the existing systems (if any) in your business. At this point, you can look for any systems that have simply emerged as "the way we do things here."

How do your staff answer the phone? What is the process customers go through when dealing with your business? How are employees hired? Trained? How is performance Reviewed and rewarded?

Some of your systems may be highly effective, and not require any changes. Others may be ineffective and require some reworking. If you have previously established some systems, now is a good time to check-in and evaluate how well they are functioning.

Use the following chart to record what systems currently exist in your business.

Existing Systems	
Administration	
Financials	
Communication	
Customer Relations	
Employees	
Marketing	
Data	

Seven Areas to Systemize

There is no doubt that system creation – especially when none exist to begin with – is a daunting and time-consuming task. For many businesses, it can be difficult to determine where to start to make the best use of their time from the onset.

Here are seven main areas of your business you can systemize. Begin with one area, and move to the other areas as you are ready. Alternately, start with one or two systems within each area, and evaluate how those new systems affect your business. Each business will require its own unique set of systems.

1. Administration

This is an important area of your business to systemize because administrative roles tend to see a high turnover. A series of systems will reduce training time, and keep you from explaining how the phones are to be answered each time a new receptionist joins your team.

Administrative Systems	
Opening and closing procedures	Filing and paper management
Phone greeting	Workflow
Mail processing	Document production
Sending couriers	Inventory management
Office maintenance (watering plants, emptying recycle bins, etc.)	Order processing
	Making orders

2. Financials

This is one area of systems that you will need to keep a close eye on – but that doesn't mean you have to do the work yourself. Financial management systems are everything from tracking credit card purchases to invoicing clients and following up on overdue accounts.

These systems will help to prevent employee theft, and allow you to always have a clear picture of your numbers. It will allow you to control purchasing, and ensure that each decision is signed-off on.

Financial Systems	
Purchasing	Profit / loss statements
Credit card purchase tracking	Invoicing
Accounts payable	Daily cash out
Accounts receivable	Petty cash
Bank deposits	Employee expenses
Cutting checks	Payroll
Tax payments	Commission payments

3. Communications

The area of communication is essential and time consuming for any business. Fax cover letters, sales letters, internal memos, reports, and newsletters are items that need to be created regularly by different people in your organization.

Most of the time, these communications aren't much different from one to the next, yet each are created from scratch by a different person. There is a huge opportunity for systemization in this area of your business. Systemized communication ensures consistency and company differentiation.

Communication Systems	
Internal memo template	Newsletter template
Fax cover template	Sales letter template(s)
Letterhead template	Meeting minutes template
Team meeting agenda	Report template
Sending faxes	Internal meetings
Internal emails	Scheduling

4. Customer Relations

Another important area for systemization is customer relations. This includes everything the customer sees or touches in your company, as well as any interaction they might have with you or your staff members.

Establishing a customer relations system will also ensure that new staff members understand how customers are handled in *your* business. It will allow you to maintain a high level of customer service, without constantly reminding staff of your policies. It will also ensure that the success of your customer relations and retention does not hinge on you or any other individual salesperson.

Customer Relations Systems	
Incoming phone call script	Sales process
Outgoing phone call script	Sales script
Customer service standards	Newsletter templates
Customer retention strategy	Ongoing customer communication strategy
Customer communications templates	
	Customer liaison policy

5. Team

Create systems in your business for hiring, training, and developing your team. This will establish clear expectations for the team members, and streamline time consuming activities like recruitment.

Employees with clear expectations who work within clear structures are happier and more productive. They are motivated to achieve 'A' when they know they will receive 'B' if they do. Establishing a clear training manual will also save you and your team the time and hassle of training each new team member on the fly.

Employee Systems	
Employee recruitment	Staff uniforms or dress code
Employee retention	Employee training
Incentive and rewards program	Ongoing training and professional development
Regular employee reviews	
Employee feedback structure	Job descriptions and role profiles

6. Marketing

This is likely an area in which you spend a large part of your time. You focus on generating new leads and getting more people to call you or walk through your doors. These efforts can be systemized and delegated to other staff members.

Use the information in this program to create simple systems for your basic promotional efforts. Any one of your staff should be able to pick up a marketing manual and implement a successful e-mail campaign or place a purposeful advertisement.

Marketing Systems	
Referral program	Regular advertisements
Customer retention program	Advertisement creation system
Regular promotions	Direct mail system
Marketing calendar	Sales procedures
Enquiries management	Lead management

7. Data

While we like to think we operate a paperless office, often the opposite is true. Your business needs to have clear systems for managing paper and electronic information to ensure that information is protected, easily accessed, and only kept when necessary.

Data management systems help you keep your office organized. Everyone knows where information is to be stored, and how it is to be handled, which prevents big stacks of paper with no place to go.

Ensure that within your data management systems you include a data backup system. That way, if anything happens to your server or computer software, your data – and potentially your business – is protected.

Data Management Systems	
IT Management	Client file system
Data backup	Project file system
Computer repairs	Point of sale system
Electronic information storage	Financial data management

Implementing New Systems

If you completed the exercise earlier in this chapter, you will have a good idea of the systems that are currently in place in your business. The next step is to determine what systems you need to create in your business.

To do this you will need to get a better understanding of the tasks that you and your employees complete on a daily and weekly basis. If you operate a timesheet program, this can be a good source of information. Alternately, ask staff to keep a daily log for a week of all the tasks they contribute to or complete. Doing so will not only give you valuable insight into their how they spend their time on a daily basis, but also involve them in the systemizing process.

Review all task logs or timesheet records at the end of the week, remove duplicates, and group like tasks together. From here you can categorize the tasks into business areas like the seven listed above, or create your own categories.

Then, you will need to prioritize and plan your system creation and implementation efforts. Choose one from each category, or one category to focus on at a time. The amount you can take on will depend on your business needs, and the staff resources you have available to you for this process.

Remember that system creation is a long-term process – not something that will transform your business overnight. Be patient, and focus on the items that hold the highest priority.

Creating Your Systems

There is a big variety of ways you can create systems for your business – depending on the type of system you need and the type of business you operate. Some systems will be short and simple – i.e., a laminated sign in the kitchen that outlines step-by-step how to make the coffee – while others will be more complex – i.e., your sales scripts or letter templates.

One thing all of your systems have in common is steps. There is a linear process involved from start to finish. Begin by writing out each of the steps involved in completing the task, and provide as much detail as you can.

Then, review your step-by-step guide with the team who regularly complete the task and gather their feedback. Once you have incorporated their input, decide what format the system needs to be in: manual, laminated instruction sheet, sign, office memo, etc.

Testing Your Systems

Now that you have created a system, you will need to make sure that it works. More specifically, you need to make sure that it works without your involvement.

Implement the new system for an appropriate period of time – a week or month – then ask for input from staff, suppliers and vendors, and customers. Evaluate if it is informative enough for your staff, seamless enough for your suppliers, and whether or not it meets or exceeds your customer's needs.

Take that feedback and revise the system accordingly. You will rarely get the system right the first time – so be patient.

Systems will also need to be evaluated and revised on a regular basis to ensure your business processes are kept up to date. Structure an annual or bi-annual review of systems, and stick to it.

Team Buy-In

It will be nearly impossible for you to develop effective systems without the involvement and input of your employees. These are the people who will be using the systems, and who are completing the tasks on a regular basis without systems. They have a wealth of knowledge to assist you in this process.

Your team can also draft the systems for you to review and finalize. This will make the systemization process a much faster and more efficient one.

It is also important to note that when you introduce new systems into your company, there may be a natural resistance to the change. People – including your team members – are habitual people who can become set in the way they are used to doing things.

Delegation

The final step to systemizing your business is delegation. What is the point of creating systems unless someone other than you can use them to perform tasks?

This doesn't have to mean completely removing your involvement from the process, but it does mean giving your employees enough freedom to complete the task within the structure of the systems you have spent time and considerable thought creating.

After that, allow yourself the freedom of focusing on the tasks that you most enjoy, and most deserve your time – like creating big picture strategies to grow your business and increase your profits.

So What Do You Do From Here?

Take Action! If you're already an accomplished entrepreneur and earning in excess of $250,000.00 per year, use this book as direction to enhance the speed of your business success. If you are not as accomplished as you would like to be then the smartest thing to do is...

A) Read This Book
B) Apply the Strategies
C) Get Around Other Freedompreneurs! (I happen to know tons of successful ones)

Concentrate on strategies to LEARN and the EARN will follow! If you are serious about taking the next step then go to work on yourself, study other business successes, understand marketing strategies and become a sponge for new (proven) material. The amazing thing about the game of entrepreneurship is that when you put proven processes to work and continue to follow them, an abundance of success will follow. The biggest mistake is to start a process and then fallback into your old habits after a short time.

Above all, get the knowledge you need before you step onto the field. Think about it... if you were going to challenge Michael Jordan to a game of H O R S E for money, wouldn't it make sense to learn the game and practice before you stepped on the court to play him? It is amazing to me how many entrepreneurs start the game of business and never become students of the craft, and first developing the necessary knowledge to be successful. Then they fail and blame the market, the economy, their location, etc. - NO BLAMING!!

If you are an entrepreneur and have not yet managed to start to create wealth and systems that allow you to take time off, travel or spend more time with your loved ones, grow your bank account or pay for your children's college, then learn and master the steps outlined in my book. I am a huge advocate of education and mentorships. Get the right information, find someone that knows how to walk you through them and watch your quality of life take new shape.

For a Free Test Drive of all my best tips, tricks and marketing resources, visit www.Freedompreneurs.club

www.ingramcontent.com/pod-product-compliance
Lightning Source LLC
Chambersburg PA
CBHW051807170526
45167CB00005B/1910